the

HOLLYWOOD SCANDAL

almanac

12 MONTHS OF SINISTER, SALACIOUS AND *SENSELESS* HISTORY!

Written by **JERRY ROBERTS**

THE
History
PRESS

Dedicated to my wife, Joanne Mallillin. Honorable mentions to James Robert Parish and the memory of Robert Mitchum.

Published by The History Press
Charleston, SC 29403
www.historypress.net

Front cover, top: Robert Mitchum in *Farewell, My Lady* (1975); *bottom*: actors playing photographers in *Woman of the Year* (1942).
Back cover: cast of *Ocean's Eleven* (1960), *from left*: Dean Martin, Frank Sinatra, Sammy Davis Jr., Joey Bishop, Peter Lawford and Angie Dickinson.

First published 2012

Manufactured in the United States

ISBN 978.1.60949.702.6

Library of Congress CIP data applied for.

Contents

Acknowledgements

This book would not be possible without the faith of The History Press administration, particularly Adam Ferrell and Brittain Phillips. I would also like to thank several colleagues at The History Press who helped me and/or put up with me in one way or another, particularly Adam Ferrell and Will McKay but also Aubrie Koenig, Becky LeJeune, Frank Travell, Annie Martz, Katie Orlando, Julie Foster, Whitney Tarella, Hannah Cassilly, Tyler Sari, Ryan Finn, Sophia Russell, Andrew Patterson, Natasha Walsh, Darcy Mahan, Jaime Muehl, Julie Scofield, Hilary Parrish, Jamie Barreto, Joe Gartrell, Ben Gibson, Katie Parry, Dan Watson, Magan Thomas, Jeff Saraceno and Chris Vaught.

I would like to thank those who have contributed images to this book or who have given their permissions to use those images, particularly friends Doug List and Don

Lechman but also Steve Takata and Richard Corso, who once operated the defunct Starline, Inc., which created the trading cards used on the following pages. The stills, publicity shots and cards all came from these four men.

When James Robert Parish was an acquisitions editor for Greenwood Press in the 1980s, he helped me to become an author. Since then, he has turned out to be the most prolific author concerning Hollywood's scandals (see the bibliography). Jim has always been an influence and an inspiration, especially for this book.

My wife, Joanne Mallillin, has been helpful in more ways than she knows. And my nephews, Kyle and Tyler Kolfschoten, have also rewarded me during this project in varying ways. Doug List, Kevin Morris, Don Lechman and Wil Haygood persist as lifelong influences. My late parents, Alex and Ann Roberts, my brother, Mark Roberts, and my cousin, Dr. Carol Grabowski, deserve some credit for keeping me honest.

Introduction

Hollywood is easy to bash. For every genuine tragedy, a dozen instances of criminal intent and sheer stupidity occur to reinforce the notion that malfeasance, wrongheadedness and sheer idiocy are more a way of life there than practically anywhere else.

For this book, an attempt was made to catalogue most of the big, well-known misadventures, disasters and boondoggles that have afflicted both the personalities associated with the screen and the movies they have foisted on us for generations. The 365 days of the year are filled in with many of the not-so-famous episodes of what Robert Mitchum once termed "untoward notoriety." On the following pages are the old and the new, the big booboos and some generally unknown stubbed toes.

The surprise of researching this book was that so many young actors in the business have exited to the great beyond.

You hear about it occasionally, that when puberty sets in, the roles dry up for former meal tickets in short pants. But when you look into it and see how many former child stars have died or just hit the skids time and again, sometimes until they do perish, some by their own hand, it's quite remarkable.

But any sadness usually gives way to a cold, hardhearted question that might be posed to nearly any one of them once they're met in that great beyond: couldn't you do anything else besides drugs and act?

The survivors are another fascination. Somewhere along the continuum of Charlie Sheen's life, as he racked up crimes and infamy, anyone might have wondered where he eventually would place in the Hollywood scandals sweeps. When Marty and Janet Sheen watched him crawl around as an infant, could there have been any inkling that this little tyke would eventually contend with Frank Sinatra for the most mentions in a book containing the 365 most scandalous episodes of Hollywood infamy?

There was a concerted effort to place an event within the context of its main date. But to fit a jigsaw puzzle such as this together and find something for every date in the calendar, it was necessary to work things around. Thus, a criminal charge or involvement has a variety of dates that can work for an entry: arrest, arraignment, release on bail, court date, trial dates, verdict, sentencing, release from jail, etc. Likewise, demise has its possibilities: death date, body found, media report, death certificate, cremation, funeral service, interment, etc.

Sins on the screen are also part of this piecemeal appreciation of Hollywood's transgressions. If you have sat through *The Swarm* (1978) or *The Jazz Singer* (1980), you have some idea of why these movies and others constitute misdeeds all their own.

Also keep in mind that times change. Divorce can still be an agonizing tragedy, although Hollywood vamps such as Elizabeth Taylor and Lana Turner helped turn its tide of shame while they also trashed the sanctity of marriage.

Alcoholism in the years between Prohibition and its late twentieth-century identity as a disease was blithely treated as an everyday way of life. But drunk driving today is recognized as the social offense it always was.

Unfasten your seat belts. It's a bumpy read, and you might as well enjoy the jostling.

JANUARY 1

1960—*HAYWIRE* IN THE END

Margaret Sullavan overdosed on sleeping pills in her room of the Taft Hotel in New Haven, Connecticut, on New Year's Day while studying for the out-of-town previews of *Sweet Love Remembered*. Her own memory lane could have used the title: she married Henry Fonda on Christmas Day 1931 and divorced him for infamously overbearing Broadway producer Jed Harris, married film director William Wyler in 1936 and traded him in for Broadway producer Leland Hayward in 1938. She divorced him to marry an investment banker. James Stewart fell hopelessly in love with her through their pictures together, including *The Shopworn Angel* (1938) and *The Shop Around the Corner* (1940). Sullavan suffered a nervous breakdown, recounted in *Haywire* (1977), her daughter's autobiography. The book became a 1980 TV movie starring Lee Remick as Margaret, whose death was ruled an accident by the New Haven County coroner. She was fifty.

JANUARY 2

1937—MAKING WAY FOR RONNIE

Warner Bros.'s favorite second lead—to Dick Powell in *Flirtation Walk* (1934), Errol Flynn in *Captain Blood* (1935) and others—Ross Alexander walked out to a familiar barn near his Hollywood home on this date. This same barn was where his twenty-two-year-old former and late wife, actress Aleta Freel, used a .22-caliber rifle to apparently shoot herself to death on December 6, 1935. Ross carried the same firearm and took his own life with it. Between apparent suicides, Ross married actress Anne Nagel. There's nothing to suggest that the reinvestigation of Aleta's death by California governor Frank Merriam at the request of New Jersey governor Harold Hoffman (she was a Jersey girl) had anything to do with Ross's gun-tote to the barn. Warner's search for Ross's replacement as the best friend *du jour* led to a Tampico, Illinois–born announcer working Chicago Cubs spring-training games on Santa Catalina Island. Ronald Reagan was screen-tested on the island, proved to be Ross's capable replacement and later dallied as president of the Screen Actors Guild, governor of California and president of the United States.

JANUARY 3

2009—BOURBON AT FAT JACK'S

Playwright and actor Sam Shepard had been into the Woodford Reserve bourbon at Fat Jack's on Main Street in Bloomington, Illinois, on this date. He even autographed a bottle of Woodford, according to bar personnel. Around 2:00 a.m., Sam was behind the wheel of a Chevy Blazer, going forty-five miles per hour in a thirty zone. The Normal, Illinois police pulled him over, arrested him for drunk driving and took him down to the McLean County Jail, where the Pulitzer Prize winner for *Buried Child* posted $300 bail. An Oscar nominee as test pilot Chuck Yeager in *The Right Stuff* (1983) and a star of such films as *Steel Magnolias* (1989) and *Black Hawk Down* (2001), Shepard, a native of Fort Sheridan, Illinois, might think twice about any more down-state drinking.

JANUARY 4

1931—SILENT STAR'S SOUND TREATMENT

Art Acord acted in the very first Hollywood feature-length film, Cecil B. De Mille's *The Squaw Man* (1914), filmed in the barn that today is the Hollywood Heritage Museum. Acord (occasionally Accord) became Universal's leading cowboy star, and his horse, Raven, was popular with kids. Their features include *The Circus Cyclone* (1925) and *Spurs and Saddles* (1927). Art's three divorces in a dozen years and gambling debts were topped by bad news: his voice wouldn't make it in the sound era. He played in a few sound films, but his star descended. A big drinker, Acord drifted into an arrest for bootlegging. Haggard from stunt work and tavern roaming, Acord expired in a Chihuahua City, Mexico, hotel room on this date. The cause of death is alternately listed as a stroke due to acute alcoholism or cyanide poisoning. He was forty.

JANUARY 5

The most irreconcilable thing left for the public by the marriage of Madonna and Sean Penn was *Shanghai Surprise* (1989). Their divorce was filed on this date, but the movie, made in 1986 in Hong Kong, was a lamebrain dud, shelved for a couple of years. Sean starred as a fortune hunter in China, with her in a vocational stretch as a missionary nurse. It cost $17 million to make and earned back $2.3 million domestically. During production, Penn infamously scuffled with a Hong Kong journalist and tried to have director Jim Goddard fired. The film company became a moveable mess, with shutterbugs colliding to get snaps of Madonna. Back in Los Angeles, songwriter David Wolinski greeted old friend Madonna with a kiss in a nightclub, and Penn went berserk, punching, kicking and clubbing the tune-meister with a chair. The couple split and reconciled in 1987 and then split for good by this date.

JANUARY 6

2011—JAMIE'S ROUGH MONTH

The 2007 Emmy Award winner for best supporting actress in *My Name Is Earl*, Jamie Pressly was amid a tough January on this date by seemingly emulating her role as the blabby peroxide-blonde bimbo Joy Turner in her NBC-TV sitcom by getting arrested for drunk driving by the Santa Monica police. Later in the month, on January 21, the former gymnast and *Playboy* model filed for divorce from Simran Singh, her entertainment lawyer husband, citing irreconcilable differences. A star of such films as *Poor White Trash* (2000), *Joe Dirt* (2001) and *I Love You, Man* (2009), Pressly pleaded no contest to the DUI on August 25, 2011, and received three years' probation.

JANUARY 7

1997—Your Cell, Madam

Disheveled and weeping, the former madam to the stars, Heidi Fleiss, was sentenced to thirty-seven months in federal prison on this date for income tax evasion and money laundering, ending one of Hollywood's more lurid actual melodramas. "The once-defiant Fleiss closed her eyes in relief," read one report, when U.S. District Court Judge Consuelo B. Marshall was lenient, slapping her with three years. During her time at the Pleasanton, California Federal Correctional Institute for Women, Fleiss was forced several times to defend herself against attacks by inmates. Originally arrested for supplying high-priced hookers and narcotics to what had been characterized as the Hollywood elite, Fleiss eventually relocated to Nye County, Nevada, keeping house with dozens of parrots.

JANUARY 8

1993—ELVIS'S POSTAGE STAMP

The U.S. Postal Service, going along with the contention that Elvis Presley died on August 16, 1977, in Memphis, Tennessee, issued on this date a stamp in memory of the King. Elvis's impact on movies was considerable, even though his often watery vehicles had the cheap look of *Gilligan's Island* episodes. He starred in thirty-one pictures, including such moving postcards as *Girls! Girls! Girls!* (1962), *Fun in Acapulco* (1963), *Viva Las Vegas* (1964), *Spinout* (1966) and *Clambake* (1967). If he wasn't exactly Olivier or Brando, he had a magnetic presence, women adored him and he could sing a little. And the facts spoke for themselves: "Presley as Top-Money Star" claimed *Variety* on July 28, 1965, and writer Vincent Canby estimated Elvis's 1965 income from movies at $2.7 million, or more than John Wayne, Cary Grant and Elizabeth Taylor. His picture for Allied Artists, *Tickle Me* (1965), saved that studio.

JANUARY 9

John Gilbert's tragedy has always been characterized as abandonment by Hollywood because his voice was judged unfit for sound pictures. But the Logan, Utah–born star was just a pain in the butt to some, pestering Metro-Goldwyn-Mayer for raises. Director King Vidor wrote that Gilbert always played a role because the person was a blank slate. A top star of his day, he fronted John Ford's *Cameo Kirby* (1923), Vidor's *The Big Parade* (1925), Erich von Stroheim's *The Merry Widow* (1925) and other big films while his boozing increased. Perhaps contrite over once leaving Gilbert at the altar, his frequent costar, Greta Garbo, insisted he costar in *Queen Christina* (1933). He made one other film, *The Captain Hates the Sea* (1934), and was to costar in *Desire* (1936) with Marlene Dietrich, but his acute alcoholism brought on a fatal heart attack on this date. He was forty.

JANUARY 10

1936—"America's Sweethearts" Go Sour

At the heart of the silent film industry's social scene was Pickfair, the Beverly Hills mansion of Mary Pickford and Douglas Fairbanks Jr. Their marriage was more internationally celebrated than actual royalty, and celestial unions since—Liz and Dick, et al.—have paled in comparison. Pickford, "America's Sweetheart," rebounded from an unhappy marriage by hitching with Fairbanks on their Liberty Bonds tour on March 28, 1920. Media darlings and significant producers, they created United Artists. Pickford won an Oscar for *Coquette* in 1929, but sound pictures finished her career. America's Sweethearts split on this date. Doug went roving to England, where he married Lady Ashley (who later married Clark Gable). Mary married Charles "Buddy" Rogers and retained Pickfair, where she parked herself within easy reach of the sideboy bar. Doug died in 1939 at age fifty-six, Mary in 1979 at eighty-seven.

JANUARY 11

The occasional firings off movie productions are mild shocks that drift quietly into trivia. Harvey Keitel was exchanged for Marty Sheen on *Apocalypse Now* (1979), and Eric Stoltz wasn't comic enough for director Bob Zemeckis on *Back to the Future* (1985), so the franchise fell to Michael J. Fox. When Robert Mitchum was fired on this date from San Francisco Bay locations for *Blood Alley* (1955)—for pranks allegedly including pushing a crew member into the bay—producer John Wayne and studio head Jack Warner replaced him with the Duke himself. It hit the papers like Big Bad Bob was the antichrist—a week of headlines during a slow January. Bob's 1947 marijuana bust was still fresh, and it didn't help that he hosted post-contretemps press interviews in his undershorts. The Duke always felt culpable in the fiasco, and the two stars eventually carried *The Longest Day* (1962) and reunited for *El Dorado* (1967).

JANUARY 12

2001—BALDWIN V. BASINGER

The eldest of the four acting Baldwin boys from Long Island, Alec Baldwin was married to Oscar winner Kim Basinger through most of the 1990s. The costars of *The Marrying Man* (1990) married in 1993 and had their daughter, Ireland, in 1995. Kim, who won an Oscar for *L.A. Confidential* (1997), filed for divorce on this date. Alec contends in his book *Promise to Ourselves* (2008), written with Mark Tabb, that Kim spent about $1.5 million to cut off any relationship with his daughter by refusing to discuss parenting, blocking visitation and telephone access, not following court orders and directly influencing the child against him. Baldwin contended he broke on April 11, 2007, when he left an angry voicemail message referring to Ireland as a "rude, thoughtless little pig," which was leaked to the TV show *TMZ*. He told *Playboy* that he contemplated suicide over the incident but instead sought professional help because he didn't want his former family to have that satisfaction. "Destroying me," he said, "was their avowed goal."

JANUARY 13

1962—So Long, Ernie Kovacs

One of Hollywood's more original comedians perished in an auto accident on this date at the corner of Santa Monica and Beverly Glen Boulevards in Los Angeles. Ernie Kovacs, a Hungarian immigrant at age thirteen and a TV comedy star who began making movies—*Our Man in Havana* (1959), *Bell, Book and Candle* (1959) and *North to Alaska* (1960)—rendezvoused with his wife and former TV costar, Edie Adams, at a baby shower for Milton Berle and his wife. Ernie and Edie left in separate cars after a rainstorm. Kovacs lost control of his Chevrolet Corvair and crashed into a phone pole. The rangy portrayer of such TV characters as Wolfgang von Sauerbraten, Auntie Gruesome, Percy Dovetonsils and Pierre Ragout was thrown partway out of the passenger side and died instantly from chest and head injuries. Jack Lemmon, who had costarred in three Ernie pictures, identified the body at the morgue after Edie broke down. Kovacs was forty-two.

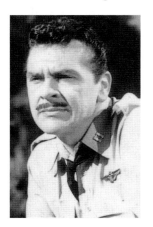

JANUARY 14

1922—CLEANING UP PICTURES

Will H. Hays resigned his cabinet position as U.S. postmaster general on this date after successfully guiding Warren G. Harding's 1920 presidential campaign. The higher office for Hays was president of the Motion Picture Producers and Distributors of America (MPPDA). A Presbyterian deacon and former chairman of the Republican National Committee, Hays began his new job at a $100,000 annual salary on March 6, 1922. The MPPDA's goal was to renovate the movie industry's image in the wake of the Fatty Arbuckle scandal, the drug death of Wallace Reid and the murder of William Desmond Taylor and to tone down the pictures as religious groups were clamoring for federal censorship. Hiring Hays, a native of Sullivan, Indiana, to "clean up the pictures" was a public relations move toward devising the Production Code in the 1930s.

JANUARY 15

1947—GO IN PIECES, MY DEAR

One of the most infamous murder cases in Hollywood or anywhere else was the killing and mutilation of unemployed waitress and aspiring actress Elizabeth Short. Her body was found surgically cut in half and drained of blood on this date in an empty lot at 3925 South Norton Avenue in South Central Los Angeles. The infamously unsolved Black Dahlia Murder has inspired many interpretations—books, films, websites, TV investigations—and speculations about call-girl rings, drinking binges, suppression of information, lost or destroyed files, police coverups and whatnot. William Randolph Hearst's newspapers, the *Los Angeles Examiner* and *Los Angeles Herald-Express*, sensationalized the case, nicknamed after the then-popular movie *The Blue Dahlia* (1946). Short has been portrayed as either a naïve innocent or an indulgent bimbo. The waters are so muddied by time that almost anything might be true. Short was twenty-two.

JANUARY 16

2008—Brad's "Stairway to Heaven"

Director Joel Schumacher had "discovered" the eleven-year-old kid from Knoxville, Tennessee, and starred him with Susan Sarandon in the film of John Grisham's *The Client* (1994). The talented upstart also starred in *Sleepers* (1996), *Apt Pupil* (1998), *Deuces Wild* (2002) and others as he literally grew up in the business. But Brad Renfro didn't last long, as acute morphine/heroin intoxication took him in his sleep on January 15, 2008. The Los Angeles County coroner ruled the death accidental. Two days before his demise, Brad had "Fuck All Ya'll" tattooed on his back. His relatives and friends paid him tribute at his grave site in Red House Cemetery in Blaine, Tennessee, on this date as Led Zeppelin's "Stairway to Heaven" played in the background. Brad was twenty-five. Two weeks later, his grandmother, Joanne, who had raised him and accompanied him to acting gigs when he was a minor, died of natural causes. She was seventy-six.

JANUARY 17

1942—LOSS OF CAROLE LOMBARD

Twenty-three minutes after refueling in Las Vegas, a TWA/Western Airlines flight carrying actress Carole Lombard, her mother, Bess Peters, and press agent Otto Winkler crashed on this date into Potosi Mountain, aka Double Up Peak, aka Table Mountain, 8,300 feet above sea level in the Spring Range of Clark County, Nevada. The three were returning from Lombard's home state of Indiana, where they had raised $2 million at a war bond rally. They were among twenty-two people aboard, including fifteen U.S. Army Air Corps pilots on what turned out to be their final flight. As soon as he heard the news, Lombard's husband, Clark Gable, flew to the site and joined the base camp as a posse of Army Air Corps personnel, Native Americans and cowboys scaled the snowy peak to find the inevitable: charred remains, fuselage and no survivors. A superb actress and sparkling comedienne, Lombard had starred in *Twentieth Century* (1934), *Nothing Sacred* (1937), *They Knew What They Wanted* (1940) and other classics. She was thirty-three.

JANUARY 18

1923—MORPHINE CLAIMS WALLY REID

Wallace Reid became involved in pictures in 1910 in Chicago, was featured in D.W. Griffith's *The Birth of a Nation* (1915) and *Intolerance* (1916) and his talent and looks, plus the abilities to write, direct and run the camera, made him an in-demand star and picture-maker. *The Roaring Road* (1919), *Double Speed* (1920) and *Excuse My Dust* (1920) were a few of his racing movies. While on location in Oregon for director James Cruze's *The Valley of the Giants* (1919), Reid was injured in a train wreck and prescribed with morphine to kill the pain. The subsequent addiction worsened at a time when rehab was nonexistent. The star couldn't kick the habit, leading to events that made the papers. Influenza resulted, and the lung and kidney congestion claimed him at the Banksia Sanitarium in Hollywood. Reid was thirty-one.

JANUARY 19

1996—DRUG-ADDLED PRODUCER

Don Simpson, the epitome of the slick Hollywood producer, was notable for the statement, "It's not how you play the game; it's how you place the blame." Successfully partnered with Jerry Bruckheimer, the duo produced *Flashdance* (1983), *Beverly Hills Cop* (1984) and *Top Gun* (1986), among others. Don was found in his Los Angeles home on this date, dead from cardiac arrest caused by narcotics. According to Charles Fleming's book, *High Concept*, Simpson spent more than $60,000 a month on pharmaceuticals. At Paramount, Simpson helped launch *Urban Cowboy* (1980), *An Officer and a Gentleman* (1982) and *48HRS* (1982) but was fired for passing out in a meeting. A harbinger of things to come occurred in 1995, when Simpson's physician, Dr. Stephen W. Ammerman, died of a drug overdose at the producer's estate. Simpson was fifty-two.

JANUARY 20

1996—HARRY DEAN'S UNWELCOME GUESTS

One of the few character actors to inspire a cult following, West Irvine, Kentucky–born Harry Dean Stanton was a gaunt presence with a hickory-smoked cadence in *Kelly's Heroes* (1970), *Farewell, My Lovely* (1975), *Repo Man* (1984) and many others. His most harrowing role was on this date, when three armed men barged into his home on Mulholland Drive in the Hollywood Hills. The actor was held prisoner by the home invaders, beaten and tied up. The none-too-bright felons stole Harry Dean's car, which was equipped with an anti-theft tracking device. Police found the vehicle in North Hollywood, staked it out and arrested the perps. Two pleaded no contest to the robbery charges and, unlike Harry Dean—whose prison pictures include *Cool Hand Luke* (1967) and *The Green Mile* (1999)—didn't get to go home at night for some time.

JANUARY 21

1959—ALFALFA, THE DEBT COLLECTOR

Carl Switzer, who played the freckle-faced, cowlick-topped Alfalfa in the *Our Gang* comedies, became a bartender, dog breeder and bear-hunting guide as an adult and handled hounds for Roy Rogers, James Stewart and Henry Fonda. In a checkered life, Switzer had been shot outside a San Fernando Valley bar and was arrested for chopping down trees in a national forest. In his final hours, he tried to collect fifty dollars for finding a dog—at night, unannounced and after drinking. The owing party was Moses "Bud" Stiltz, who had been hired by the famed stunt man and restaurateur Ray "Crash" Corrigan after the latter received death threats. Crash's wife, Rita, was present with her son, Tom, during the attempted debt collection. Bud pulled a gun after Switzer threatened to kill him. During a scuffle, Switzer was shot in the stomach. He died on the operating table. An inquest ruled the death justifiable homicide. Switzer was thirty-two.

JANUARY 22

Heath Ledger was found unconscious in his SoHo, Manhattan apartment on this date. Masseuse Diana Lee Wolozin arrived early for a 3:00 p.m. appointment, found the actor in bed and unresponsive and telephoned Ledger's friend, Mary Kate Olsen. The actress, of "Olsen twins" fame, told a New York City private security guard to go investigate. At 3:26 p.m., acting on her fear that Ledger was dead, Wolozin called 911, and the emergency operator advised CPR, which was unsuccessful. The security guard and EMTs arrived simultaneously, but the technicians were unable to resuscitate the star of *The Patriot* (2000), *Brokeback Mountain* (2005), *The Dark Knight* (2008) and other films. He was pronounced dead at 3:36 p.m. The New York County coroner's report concluded that Ledger died of acute intoxication from a combination of oxycodone, hydrocodone, diazepam, temazepam, alprazolam and doxylamine—from an accidental overdose. Ledger posthumously won the Oscar for best supporting actor as the Joker in *The Dark Knight*. He was twenty-eight.

JANUARY 23

1990—Charlie Sheen Says He Lied

Charlie Sheen supposedly shot his fiancée, Kelly Preston, in the arm at their Malibu luxury town house on this date. She was treated by paramedics and taken to St. John's Medical Center in Santa Monica, where injuries to her wrist and ankle were treated. Charlie accepted responsibility, and the couple split up. More than two decades after the fact—or, apparently in this case, fib—Sheen said he never shot Preston. During the Vancouver stop of Charlie's crackpot 2011 "Violent Torpedo of Truth" tour, he said that Preston, in the bathroom of their Malibu condo, picked up a pair of his pants, and a revolver fell out, discharging when it hit the floor. The bullet ricocheted off the toilet. The porcelain chips hit Kelly in the arm. Charlie staunched the bleeding, called the paramedics and took the blame for her injury. Preston, an actress in *Secret Admirer* (1985) and *52-Pickup* (1986), married John Travolta in 1991.

JANUARY 24

2006—CHRIS PENN'S DEATH A SHOCKER

Although his older brother, Sean Penn, usually grabbed the headlines for both on- and off-screen performances, character actor Christopher Penn picked up the notices on this date when he was found dead in his Santa Monica condominium. A drinker and recreational drug user, Penn died of unspecified heart disease (cardiomyopathy). Codeine and promethazine were in his system, according to the Los Angeles County coroner, and he had an enlarged heart. Chris Penn's excess weight added to his menacing presence in later roles, and he was memorable as Nice Guy Eddie in Quentin Tarantino's *Reservoir Dogs* (1992) and as Nicky Dimes in *True Romance* (1993). Sean said that his brother's weight probably led to his death. Chris Penn was forty.

JANUARY 25

1966—MICK'S FIFTH ONE A DOOZY

Mickey Rooney filed for his fifth divorce the day before this date, recovering in St. John's Hospital in Santa Monica from an intestinal malady contracted in the Philippines while filming *Ambush Bay*. His wife Barbara's affair with Milos Milosevic, aka "Milos Milos," a Serbian who costarred in *Incubus* (1966) and *The Russians Are Coming, the Russians Are*

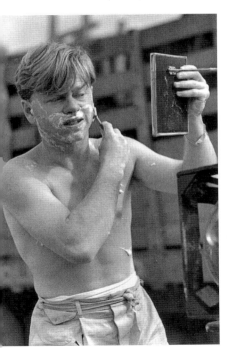

Coming (1966), was the reason for Mick's action. Barbara Ann Thomason Rooney, at age seventeen in 1954, had been Miss Muscle Beach, Miss Bay Beach and Miss Surfestival and, as "Carolyn Mitchell," appeared in Roger Corman's 1958 films *Dragstrip Riot* and *Cry Baby Killer*. On January 31, the Rooneys' maid found the bodies of Milos and Barbara on the bathroom floor of Mick's master bedroom. Milos apparently had shot her in the face and then turned the gun on himself. She was twenty-nine, he twenty-four.

JANUARY 26

1971—MANSON FAMILY VALUES

News reached middle America on this date that Charles Manson and his cult followers Susan Atkins, Patricia Krenwinkel and Leslie Van Houten were found guilty of each of the twenty-seven separate counts of murder and conspiracy in the Tate-LaBianca murders. Two Los Angeles–area households had been attacked by the Manson cult "family," and pregnant actress Sharon Tate, who costarred in husband Roman Polanski's *The Fearless Vampire Killers* (1967) as well as *Valley of the Dolls* (1967) and *The Wrecking Crew* (1967), was among the victims. Midway through the penalty phase, Manson shaved his head and trimmed his beard to a fork. "I am the devil, and the devil always has a bald head," he told the press. On March 29, the jury returned verdicts of death against all four defendants on all counts, sentences affirmed by Judge Charles H. "Chuck" Older. Manson remains in prison due to California's impasse on the death penalty, and his follower, Lynette "Squeaky" Fromme, attempted to assassinate President Gerald Ford in Sacramento in 1975.

JANUARY 27

1973—NEW USE FOR BUTTER

The larder staple became part of the boudoir banquet—if you could call it that—at the demand of despairing widower Marlon Brando to facilitate lovemaking with willing Parisian Maria Schneider as they couple again and again in director Bernardo Bertolucci's controversial psycho-sexual classic, *Last Tango in Paris*. It was released on this date in New York and London before wide distribution in February. *New Yorker* critic Pauline Kael likened the event to a benchmark in the arts, and the advance publicity, emphasizing the critical praise and extended sexual sequences, made the picture more than just a curio of its time. Brando's astonishing performance garnered an Oscar nomination, but Jack Lemmon won the bauble for *Save the Tiger* (1973). The dairy industry never did capitalize on the opportunity.

JANUARY 28

1984—BABS BAGS BAUBLE

The first question during the lie detector test that should have been administered to the Hollywood Foreign Press Association after the Golden Globes were awarded on this date would have been: did you actually sit through all 134 can-cramping, snore-forcing minutes of Barbra Streisand's *Yentl*? The picture about an Eastern European teen girl impersonating a man to get an education was a Barbra barbarity, a Babs-ballyhooing Babs-a-thon Babs-fest from A through Babs, all Babs all the time—cowritten by Babs, directed by Babs, produced by Babs and starring Babs. It was the most Babs-arific Babs-tacular ever—*the* vanity project of all time, bar none. *Yentl* also got Globe nominations for best musical/comedy and for Babs for best actress for playing a teen at age forty-one— talk about acting. (The film won the Oscar for best score and received five nominations.) In gaining the Globe for best director, Babs beat out slouches Ingmar Bergman, Mike Nichols, James L. Brooks, Bruce Beresford and Peter Yates.

JANUARY 29

1964—No Coming Back

The star of *This Gun for Hire* (1942), *The Blue Dahlia* (1946) and *Shane* (1953) was found dead in Palm Springs on this date. Alan Ladd's cocktail of exit was alcohol, three medicines and sleeping pills. He had just finished filming one of his bigger hits, *The Carpetbaggers* (1964), after failing to transcend the living two years earlier when he was found in a pool of blood with a bullet wound near his heart. Suspicions were that he was a closeted gay man in an era when homosexuality wasn't accepted in mainstream Hollywood, hastening his goodbye. He was fifty. Ladd's mother had committed suicide, and the actor married his agent, Sue Carol. His name lived on: Alan Ladd Jr.,

aka "Laddie," the actor's son by his first marriage to Marjorie Harrold, produced the Oscar-winning best pictures *Chariots of Fire* (1981) and *Braveheart* (1993). Jordan Ladd, the daughter of Alan Sr.'s other son, David, and actress Cheryl Ladd of *Charlie's Angels* TV fame, was in Quentin Tarantino's *Grindhouse* (2007) and other films.

JANUARY 30

1982—THE WINNER IS...PIA ZADORA?!

The diminutive blonde *Playboy* model and Las Vegas performer Pia Zadora won the New Star of the Year Award in Motion Pictures at the annual Golden Globes in the Beverly Hilton Hotel on this date. *Pia who?* Her movie was *Butterfly*, which hadn't yet been released in the United States. She won the New Star bauble over Kathleen Turner in *Body Heat* and Howard E. Rollins in *Ragtime*. The truth was that the twenty-six-year-old's tycoon husband, Meshulam Riklis, fifty-eight, owner of the Riviera Hotel in Las Vegas, had wined and dined the Hollywood Foreign Press Association (HFPA), purveyors of the Golden Globes, at both his Nevada hotel on November 4, 1981, and his Beverly Hills mansion. He produced *Butterfly*, a trashy little item of backwoods seduction, and bought off the HFPA to award a performer in a film its members had not yet seen. The Federal Communications Commission was miffed at this influence peddling, and NBC-TV took the Globes off the air.

JANUARY 31

1957—THE LIZ TAYLOR TRADITION

Divorce was one of Lizzie's specialties. The violet-eyed teenage beauty was divorced from hotel heir Conrad Nicholson "Nicky" Hilton Jr. and had gone through the Howard Hughes dating ritual by the time she oiled up the detachment process from her second hubby, actor Michael Wilding. She was nineteen and

Wilding thirty-nine when they met in England during filming on *Ivanhoe* (1952). They married on February 21, 1952, and had two children, but the union faded after she went to Texas to make director George Stevens's *Giant* (1956). Wilding's aristocratic charm propelled him through such films as *In Which We Serve* (1942), *Under Capricorn* (1949) and *The Naked Edge* (1961), but he couldn't keep a hot, man-hungry dame like Liz tied down. The Wildings separated in July 1956, and Liz latched onto film producer Mike Todd before the divorce was inked.

FEBRUARY 1

2010—RIP TORN, RIPPED AGAIN

Rip Torn was arrested on January 29, 2010, after breaking into a closed Litchfield Bancorp branch in Salisbury, Connecticut. According to reports, Torn went to sleep in the bank and asked police what they were doing in his house when they arrived. An Emmy winner in 1996 for *The Larry Sanders Show* and an Oscar nominee for *Cross Creek* (1983), the Ripster was charged with carrying a firearm without a permit and while intoxicated, burglary, criminal trespassing and criminal mischief. Torn appeared in court on this date, a few days shy of his eightieth birthday (on February 6), and his attorney told the judge that his client needed help with alcohol abuse. Elmore Rual Torn Jr., originally from Temple, Texas, was released on $100,000 bail and told to enter evaluation for substance abuse. In 2009, Torn was given probation in a Connecticut drunk-driving case and also was arrested twice on DUIs in New York.

FEBRUARY 2

1922—DEAD DIRECTOR CAPER

William Desmond Taylor's demise remains one of Hollywood's most mystifying unsolved murders. A successful Hollywood director of more than fifty pictures from 1914, his films included vehicles for silent stars Constance Talmadge, Mary Miles Minter and Mary Pickford. Taylor's body was found in his Hollywood home on this date with a bullet in his back. A gunshot was heard during the night. The inquest produced witnesses who said a young, dark-haired man left Taylor's house the night of February 1. No one was arrested. One theory held that Taylor, who was dating actress Mabel Normand, hated her cocaine habit, and pushers did him in. Born William Cunningham Deane-Tanner in 1872 in Carlow, Ireland, Taylor had immigrated to New York, married a Wall Street financier's daughter, fathered a daughter and was a member of high society. In 1908, he mysteriously disappeared from New York and turned up in Hollywood six years later. *Taylorology*, a fanzine based at the University of Arizona, kept up interest in the case in the 1990s.

FEBRUARY 3

1991—*LITTLE GIRL LOST*

Drew Barrymore got an early and big start in movies at age seven with director Steven Spielberg's *E. T.: The Extra-Terrestrial* (1982) and then starred in the film of Stephen King's *Firestarter* (1984). She took a similar early and big approach to abusing addictive substances: booze at age nine, marijuana at ten and cocaine at twelve. She covered this girlhood in one of the best autobiographies about drug addiction, *Little Girl Lost*, released by Pocket Books this week. Back in the employment groove and exploiting her street rep in *Poison Ivy* (1992) and *Bad Girls* (1994), the daughter of John Drew Barrymore and granddaughter of John Barrymore (and grandniece of Ethel and Lionel) not only built a fan base and a reputation as a solid, attractive, viable and smart star performer, but she also became a producer of some note and a bankable leading lady, getting $14 million for *Charlie's Angels: Full Throttle* (2003). She beat the odds faced by most narcotics-addled losers—so far.

FEBRUARY 4

1961—*MISFITS* KILLS "THE KING"

Director John Huston assembled an outstanding cast to film playwright Arthur Miller's original screenplay about a depressed divorcée and a group of cowboy chumps in the Nevada desert: Clark Gable, Marilyn Monroe, Montgomery Clift, Eli Wallach, Thelma Ritter and Kevin McCarthy. They all did the production proud, illuminating contemplative characters and a pokey story with quiet ease. Miller's wife, Monroe, customarily delayed production even as the mortality rate sped up. *The Misfits*, which was in its first week of release on this date, was already known as the film that, loosely speaking, killed Gable. He died before it was released, on November 16, 1960, of coronary thrombosis after a heart attack. Marilyn expired rather infamously two years later, on August 5, 1962. And Monty held out until July 23, 1966.

FEBRUARY 5

1943—*THE OUTLAW* RELEASED

Jane Russell was nineteen when Howard Hughes signed her to a seven-year contract in 1940 and starred her in a western ostensibly about Billy the Kid. Actually, it was really about her anatomy. Hughes took the project over from director Howard Hawks and lit many scenes himself that presented Russell as Rio, Doc Holliday's fictional girlfriend. Hughes engineered a new cantilevered underwire bra for that bulging effect—a pre-3-D effort on a 40-D-D subject. Russell deceived Hughes by never wearing his bra. A film that normally should have been shot and processed in a couple of months was released on this date after nearly four years of Hughes's mammary obsession. "What are the two great reasons for Jane Russell's rise to stardom?" asked the

advertising, depicting Jane in a flimsy blouse. Denied the Production Code seal of approval, *The Outlaw* was condemned by the National Legion of Decency. Hughes released it in San Francisco on this date. Other edited versions were distributed in 1946 and 1947. Russell became a star in her own right in such films as *Macao* (1952) and *Gentlemen Prefer Blondes* (1953).

FEBRUARY 6

1943—TASMANIAN DEVIL ACQUITTED

After a sensational trial lasting nearly a month, the movies' greatest swashbuckler, Errol Flynn, star of *Captain Blood* (1935), *The Charge of the Light Brigade* (1936), *The Adventures of Robin Hood* (1938) and other instant classics, was acquitted on this date of two counts of statutory rape, one supposedly aboard his yacht at Catalina and one in his Los Angeles bedroom. Employing lawyer-to-the-stars Jerry Geisler, the native Tasmanian Flynn watched as the jury of mostly women heard conflicting stories from the girls, one of whom admitted to previous sexual relations with men, and eventually voted to have the charges dropped. Between the actor's October arrest and acquittal, the papers brought the actor's hard-drinking, womanizing life under close scrutiny. Flynn's eleven-acre estate was invaded by trespassers, and the barroom slang "jail bait" and "San Quentin quail" were illuminated for America, while "in like Flynn" entered the macho lexicon. Flynn continued as a big star, including in *The Adventures of Don Juan* (1948).

Errol Flynn (right) fenced with Basil Rathbone in *The Adventures of Robin Hood* (1938).

FEBRUARY 7

1968—COCKTAIL TO THE BEYOND

Nicholas Aloysius Adamshock of Nanticoke, Pennsylvania, was ubiquitous in the 1950s, in *Mister Roberts* (1955), *Picnic* (1955), *No Time for Sergeants* (1958) and the Civil War series *The Rebel*, which he created and wrote for ABC-TV from 1959 to 1962. Adams's friendships with James Dean, Elvis Presley and Natalie Wood deepened a cult of speculation after his death. Because of his closeness to the bisexual Dean, Adams was also pegged as gay in a Hollywood era when homosexuality was largely closeted. Adams's lawyer, Erwin Roeder, drove to the actor's Beverly Hills home on this date and discovered Nick's body slumped against a bedroom wall. The Los Angeles County coroner attributed Adams's end to a toxic combination of paraldehyde and promazine. Other drugs were present in the actor's system, but the death was never concluded to be a suicide. Adams was thirty-six.

FEBRUARY 8

1994—BIG JACK ATTACK: FORE!

Oscar winner Jack Nicholson jumped out of his Mercedes-Benz at the corner of Riverside Drive and Moorpark Street in Studio City, near the Lakeside Golf Course, on this date and attacked motorist Robert Blank's Mercedes-Benz with a golf club. The actor felt that Blank cut him off in traffic. After smashing the car's windshield and denting its roof, Jack, apparently having a below-par day, drove away. Nicholson was charged with misdemeanor assault and vandalism, and Blank sued him, claiming assault and battery. The civil suit was settled out of court, and the criminal case was dropped. In his defense, Jack maintained that a good friend had just died, plus he had been up all night playing a wolf-man type of killer in director Mike Nichols's *Wolf* (1994). This sudden episode of road rage didn't stunt Jack's popularity: he won his third Oscar three years later playing a cynical, phobia-obsessed neighbor in *As Good as It Gets* (1997).

FEBRUARY 9

1944—RIGHT OF RIGHT WING

The Commies were infiltrating Hollywood and the American way of life was at stake, according to the Motion Picture Alliance for the Preservation of American Ideals (MPAPA), which was announced by *Variety* on this date. Believing in liberty and freedom, the organization said, "We find ourselves in sharp revolt against a rising tide of communism, fascism, and kindred beliefs, that [*sic*] seek by subversive means to undermine and change this way of life." Director Sam Wood was the first president, and John Ford cronies Ward Bond, John Wayne and screenwriter James Kevin McGuinness were involved, as were Walt Disney and directors King Vidor and Leo McCarey. Wayne was installed as president in 1948, and the Duke put his money where his mouth was, producing and starring in the way-laughable anti-Commie crusade *Big Jim McLain* (1952). The MPAPA supported the efforts of Senator Joseph McCarthy and publisher Billy Wilkerson's right-wing *Hollywood Reporter* to ferret out Commies in the movie business. After McCarthy's accusations ruined many careers, the MPAPA drifted into obscurity.

FEBRUARY 10

2004—PARALYZED, AND REALLY PARALYZED

The day after the California Highway Patrol said it would seek a felony DUI charge against Robert Conrad, the one-time star of television's *Wild, Wild West* lost a bit of his ersatz western cool with some body control. Conrad, sixty-nine, was buzzing along in his Jaguar near his home in Calaveras County in March 2003 when he lost control, swerved across the double-yellow line of Highway 4 and slammed head-on into a Subaru. Kevin Burnett, the Subaru driver, was hospitalized with a broken wrist and leg. Bob had three times the alcohol in his bloodstream allowable by California law. To avoid prison, the star of the series *Hawaiian Eye* and *Black Sheep Squadron*, as well as the films *Murph the Surf* (1975) and *Samurai Cowboy* (1994), worked out a deal by changing his plea from not guilty to no contest. He received six months of house arrest, five years' probation and $4,000 in fines and restitution. He remains partially paralyzed. Burnett's civil suit against Conrad was settled out of court. Burnett died in 2005 from perforated ulcers, which his family attributed to the trauma. He was twenty-eight.

FEBRUARY 11

2012—WHITNEY'S FINAL CURTAIN

One of the bigger recording artists of her time and the star of such films as *The Bodyguard* (1992), *Waiting to Exhale* (1995) and *The Preacher's Wife* (1996), Whitney Houston also battled drug addiction for much of her adult life. Her central domestic relationship, with rapper Bobby Brown, was boulder-strewn at best. Her life's journey was infamously cut short on this date. Whitney's body was found submerged in a bathtub in Suite 434 of the Beverly Hilton Hotel. The Los Angeles County coroner ruled the death a drowning accident with the "effects of atherosclerotic heart disease and cocaine use." The finding also reported that she had used cocaine shortly before her death. A memorial was held on February 18, 2012, at the New Hope Baptist Church in her native Newark, New Jersey. Whitney was forty-eight.

FEBRUARY 12

1976—MURDER WITHOUT A CAUSE

Returning to his West Hollywood apartment on this date, Sal Mineo parked his blue Chevelle in the garage at about 11:30 p.m., when his neighbors, Raymond Evans and the mother of lawyer-to-the-stars Marvin Mitchelson (the apartment building's owner), heard his screams from the back alley: "Help! Help! *Oh, my God!*" Evans rushed to the alley and found Sal in a pool of blood, stabbed in the heart. Evans's mouth-to-mouth resuscitation was futile. After a few gasps, Sal was dead. Mineo, who received Oscar nominations for director Nicholas Ray's *Rebel Without a Cause* (1955) and Otto Preminger's *Exodus* (1960), wasn't robbed, and no evidence pointed to sexual solicitation. One Lionel Ray Williams, a former pizza deliveryman serving time in Michigan for check fraud, bragged about the Mineo murder, saying he didn't know who Sal was at the time. Eventually, Williams was sentenced to fifty-seven years in the Mineo case and for eleven robberies in the same area. A strikingly similar unsolved murder occurred in the neighborhood exactly one year later, on February 12, 1977, that of actress Christa Helm. Sal was thirty-seven.

FEBRUARY 13

1958—EARLY STAR ENDS IT ALL

Helen Twelvetrees had starred in some big films, including *The Painted Desert* (1931) and *Now I'll Tell* (1934) with Spencer Tracy and Shirley Temple, but her career dipped to B westerns. Her third marriage after actors Jack Woody and Clark Twelvetrees was to career serviceman Conrad Payne. After she had left Hollywood behind, Helen was found unresponsive on the floor of her living room on this date in a modest bungalow located on Oak Hill Drive in Harrisburg, Pennsylvania. In what was ruled a suicide by the Dauphin County coroner, Helen's official cause of death was an overdose of prescription medication for a chronic kidney ailment. Her cremated remains were interred several months after her death in Middletown Cemetery in a funeral attended only by her husband and a close friend. Her burial plot was left unmarked and considered "lost" until it was rediscovered in 2009. She was forty-nine.

FEBRUARY 14

1939—CUKOR GONE WITH THE WIND

The biggest film production that Hollywood had yet seen halted and changed artistic drivers in mid-production on this date as Victor Fleming replaced George Cukor as director of producer David O. Selznick's gigantic Civil War–era drama, *Gone with the Wind*. The adaptation of Margaret Mitchell's epic novel starred Clark Gable and Vivien Leigh. Three weeks into production, Selznick decided to dump Cukor, who actually was bored by two years of preparation on the script and pre-production. Fleming, who was pulled off *The Wizard of Oz* (1939) for the reassignment and received sole final credit on *Gone with the Wind*, was himself replaced for two weeks that May by Sam Wood, due to the former's exhaustion. Fleming finished the picture, which won eight Oscars, including for best picture, director, actress (Leigh) and supporting actress—Hattie McDaniel, the first African American to win an acting Academy Award.

FEBRUARY 15

1995—Sonja Davis's Last Jump

The stunt was a forty-two-foot fall in a narrow alley on November 3, 1994. Veteran stuntwoman Sonja Davis, doubling for Angela Bassett in a scene from *Vampire in Brooklyn* (1995), landed on the air bag, but her head hit the cement next to the bag, causing massive head trauma. The actress and stuntwoman, who had performed stunts for Janet Jackson and Whoopi Goldberg, expired on November 14, 1994. The California Department of Industrial Relations, Division of Occupational Safety and Health (Cal/OSHA), issued four citations to Paramount Pictures after investigating the fatality, including the failure to ensure Davis was properly trained and the use of an air bag that was "not adequate for the purpose of the stunt being performed." No emergency medical presence was at the filming site, just a nurse. EMTs arrived after fifteen minutes. Davis died eleven days later. Swashbuckling attorney Melvin Belli, who had defended Muhammad Ali and Mae West, filed a $10 million wrongful death and distress lawsuit on behalf of Davis's family this week against Paramount Pictures, producer-star Eddie Murphy, director Wes Craven, stunt coordinator Alan Oliney and ten others. Paramount officials never commented on the suit, which presumably was settled out of court.

FEBRUARY 16

Activists Tom Hayden and Jane Fonda—the perfect sweethearts of the political left and the first couple of LA's Westside—were divorced on this date after sixteen years of marriage. A former California state senator and state assemblyman, Hayden's street cred came from drafting the Port Huron manifesto for the New Left political agenda of the 1960s. He had been a freedom rider on racially segregated buses in the Deep South during the civil rights movement and was one of the infamous Chicago Eight who were convicted of crossing state lines to incite a riot at the 1968 Democratic National Convention—a conviction overturned on appeal. His trophy wife had been a double Oscar winner for *Klute* (1971) and *Coming Home* (1978) and a fellow traveler to North Vietnam during the Vietnam War on antiwar protest efforts. She had segued into exercise videos as a means of continuing celebrity. That stardom was further promulgated by her post-Hayden union with media mogul and Atlanta Braves owner Ted Turner. Hayden's follow-up was a marriage to actress Barbara Williams, whose films include John Sayles's *City of Hope* (1991).

FEBRUARY 17

2007—BOOK THROWN AT PARIS

Heiress, occasional actress and a tall blonde who has somehow stayed famous from previously being famous—on TV, through autobiographies (not kidding) and recordings, in a bootleg celeb sex tape and such movies as *Pledge This!* (2006) and *The Hottie & the Nottie* (2008)—Paris Hilton was pulled over by the cops again on this date. She was speeding in a blue Bentley on Sunset Boulevard without the headlights on after dark and driving with a suspended license. This parole violation for a September 2006 DUI prompted a judge to sentence her to forty-five days in the Century Regional Detention Center in Lynwood, California. Her psychiatrist claimed she was on the verge of a nervous breakdown, so she was returned to her Kings Road home with an electronic ankle bracelet confining her to her house. "Special treatment!" came the protests in this case for a filthy rich, platinum-blonde bimbo of barely detectable talents. Paris was hauled back to court in handcuffs and ordered back to her cell. She was released, after serving her time, on June 27. Paris since has been busted twice for drug possession.

FEBRUARY 18

1978—MAGGIE MAKES AN EXIT

Maggie McNamara received an Oscar nomination for best actress for director Otto Preminger's *The Moon Is Blue* (1950), which caused controversy for the use of such previously taboo words on the screen as "virgin" and "pregnant." A model who also acted on Broadway, Maggie starred in the films *Three Coins in the Fountain* (1954) and *The Prince of Players* (1955), and Preminger gave her a role in *The Cardinal* (1963) as her Hollywood career seemed to dwindle away. She was married in the 1950s to prolific screenwriter and director David Swift. The marriage ended in divorce, and McNamara stayed single the rest of her rather short life. After a few TV guest spots, her last onscreen role occurred in 1964. She subsequently worked as a typist in New York City. She was found dead on this date after a deliberate overdose of sleeping pills. She left a suicide note. Maggie is buried in St. Charles Cemetery in Farmingdale, Long Island, New York. She was forty-eight.

FEBRUARY 19

1972—SAMMY SMOOCHES ARCHIE

Archie Bunker, the blue-collar, blowhard bigot played by Carroll O'Connor on the influential sitcom *All in the Family*, had one of his biggest surprises on this date, along with America at large. With the nation still healing from racist antagonisms in the years after President Lyndon Johnson signed civil rights legislation into law in the 1960s, black-white relations were tenuous at best. Sammy Davis Jr., the world's most famous black, one-eyed Jew, was the guest star on this date as himself, getting a taxi ride from Archie, who moonlighted as a cabbie. The producers wanted this episode of black-white byplay between the singing movie and nightclub star and the language-mangling bigot to have a zinger at the close. Director John Rich suggested that Sammy kiss Archie. The moment, according to the late Rich, "earned us the biggest, longest laugh I have ever experienced." O'Connor's shocked look is a moment out of TV history.

FEBRUARY 20

1997—BEING CHARLIE'S GIRLFRIEND

Brittany Ashland, who has acted in adult films as Tanya Rivers, filed a lawsuit against Charlie Sheen on February 6, 1997, claiming that on December 20, 1996, the actor grabbed her by her hair and slammed her onto the marble floor of his Agoura Hills, California, home. She was knocked unconscious and split her lip, an injury requiring seven stitches. The suit also claimed that Sheen forced her to strip and dispose of her bloody clothes. She said he threatened to kill her if she told anyone about the assault. The suit charged the actor with assault, battery, negligence, false imprisonment and emotional distress. Police investigated the claim, and prosecutors filed criminal charges against the actor on this date for misdemeanor battery with serious injury. Sheen initially pleaded not guilty, but on June 7, 1997, he entered a plea of no contest and was sentenced to a one-year suspended prison term and two years' probation and ordered to pay $2,800 in fines and restitution, perform community service and attend counseling.

FEBRUARY 21

1998—LIFE IMITATES BAD "ART"

The name Alan Smithee was concocted by the Directors
Guild of America as an alias for directors whose films
met with "moral foul play" after they delivered them to
studios, which usually have been blamed in such cases
for meddlesome editing. After screenwriter Joe Eszterhas
cooked up a Hollywood insider screenplay about a director
who seeks the moniker on his own terrible movie, that
movie was so terrible that the director, Arthur Hiller,
sought the Alan Smithee credit on the Alan Smithee film.
An Alan Smithee Film: Burn, Baby, Burn! was released this week
and sank like a lead duck at the box office. It was another
example of Hollywood big shots blowing dough on a film-
biz insider joke padded out to eighty-six minutes that no
one beyond trivia nuts, and not even them, cared one iota
about. Eric Idle played the Alan Smithee director in the
film, and going down with the ship were Ryan O'Neal,
Sandra Bernhard, Coolio and, in cameos, Sylvester
Stallone, Whoopi Goldberg, Bob Evans and Peter Bart,
among others.

FEBRUARY 22

1958—GET THE SHOW ON THE ROAD

Frank Sinatra and a few of his pals were fed up on this night with getting their posteriors cramped at the Golden Globes Awards ceremony. They sat and rolled their peepers as Zsa Zsa Gabor, whose only film that year was the B picture *The Girl in the Kremlin*, won a one-time bauble as "Most Glamorous Actress." Other glitzy shenanigans played out before Frank picked up his hardware for best actor in a musical/comedy, for director George Sidney's *Pal Joey*. As chairman of the board of that unofficial party-hearty crowd, the Rat Pack, Frank used the opportunity to gas up the shindig for the clowns in charge. He helped dole out the hardware bing-bang-boom! The boozy crowd perked up, and the Hollywood Foreign Press Association, which gives out the Golden Globes, was so impressed with this razzmatazz that it asked Frank and Dino (Dean Martin) to host the Golden Globes the following year, which they did.

FEBRUARY 23

2000—HALLE'S HITS AVOID "-AND-RUN"

Halle Berry's decision at Sunset Boulevard and Doheny Drive in a rented Chevrolet Blazer on this date wasn't among her great choices. Berry allegedly ran a red light, smashed into another car and kept going, suffering a gash on her forehead that required twenty sutures. This was a mitigating circumstance in a misdemeanor charge of leaving an accident scene filed against her, rather than a hit-and-run felony. She told a police officer at the hospital about the crash. The other car's driver sustained a broken wrist and sued. Investigators found no evidence of alcohol or drugs. Halle pleaded no contest and received three years' probation, paid $14,000 in fines and performed two hundred hours of community service. She had just won an Emmy Award and Golden Globe as best actress for *Introducing Dorothy Dandridge* (1999) and survived the ordeal to win the best actress Oscar for *Monster's Ball* (2001).

FEBRUARY 24

2008—Oscar Boycotts Avoided

The eightieth Academy Awards ceremony proceeded as normal on this date from the Kodak Theatre in Hollywood via ABC-TV's international feed, with Jon Stewart as host and the Coen brothers' *No Country for Old Men* winning the best picture statuette. The Oscars went off without a hitch, providing an anticlimactic end to uncertainty created by a Writers Guild of America (WGA) strike in the preceding months—lifted less than two weeks prior to this night. Long-term planning for the show had been a nightmare. On December 18, 2007, the striking WGA denied a waiver requested by the Academy of Motion Picture Arts & Sciences in connection with film clips and excerpts from previous award ceremonies to be shown at the 2008 awards. Anticipating that the strike would continue through Oscar Night, the academy developed a plan B show that would not have included actors. The Screen Actors Guild vowed solidarity for its striking counterpart. On February 12, a deal reached by the WGA and the Alliance of Motion Picture and Television Producers ended months of alternative planning and gnashing of teeth.

FEBRUARY 25

1996—KILLING FIELDS CAN FIND YOU

This time, the fatality's locale was 945 North Beaudry Avenue in downtown Los Angeles, in the hilly neighborhood between Chinatown and Dodger Stadium. Until this date, the victim was one of the most internationally famous survivors of his time. Dr. Haing S. Ngor—the Cambodian physician who enacted the tragic and danger-fraught story of Dith Pran, opposite Sam Waterston as *New York Times* war correspondent Sydney Schanberg, in *The Killing Fields* (1984)—was shot to death in the driveway of his home. Ngor had won the Oscar as best supporting actor of 1984, playing Pran, a fellow Khmer Rouge survivor. Ngor was murdered by street gang members because he refused to give up a gold locket containing a picture of his late wife, who had been allowed to die in childbirth by ruthless Khmer Rouge soldiers in the actual killing fields of 1975. The locket was never recovered. Ngor was fifty-five.

FEBRUARY 26

2004—Christ, Controversy, Coffers

The day after Ash Wednesday and the release of director Mel Gibson's *The Passion of the Christ*, a rather hardhearted, dour and bloody rendition of the *Passion Play*, the critics complained of the deviations from scripture, the use of perhaps more gore than was necessary and an undercurrent of anti-Semitism in the screenplay by Benedict Fitzgerald and Mr. Mel himself. Starring Jim Caviezel as Jesus, the film out-scandalized the last scandalous film on the same subject, Martin Scorsese's *The Last Temptation of Christ* (1988). Writing in the *New Republic*, Leon Wieseltier averred of Gibson's film, "These are not merely anti-Semitic images; these are classically anti-Semitic images." The movie was nominated for three below-the-line Oscars, including Caleb Deschanel's cinematography. The real shock of the enterprise was that it grossed $600 million in theatrical release, the biggest take of any R-rated film up to that time.

FEBRUARY 27

The second installment of "Raising Kane," a two-part essay by Pauline Kael in the *New Yorker*, held that Herman J. Mankiewicz, who shared with Orson Welles the screenplay credit for America's great cinematic masterpiece, *Citizen Kane* (1941), was, in fact, the great unsung creative force behind the film. She presented this case for Mankiewicz more than a decade after his death and against the tide of the obvious: the film was directed and produced by Welles, who starred as Kane. Kael went so far as to say Mankiewicz wrote almost the entire script, with only minor alterations by Welles, and that Welles not only tried to hog sole credit for the screenplay but also tried to bribe Manky off the byline. Atlantic Monthly Press and Little, Brown combined to package the original screenplay with the essay into *The Citizen Kane Book*, and this malarkey sits yet on library shelves. Welles scholars, including Peter Bogdanovich, Andrew Sarris, Joseph McBride and Jonathan Rosenbaum, have refuted the Kael blasphemy to little avail. Kael succeeded in her quest to be film criticism's queen provocateur.

FEBRUARY 28

1991—CHRISTIAN BRANDO SENTENCED

The eldest son of Marlon Brando was sentenced to ten years in state prison on this date for shooting Dag Drollet, the boyfriend of the son's half sister, Cheyenne Brando. Drollet was gunned down in the paterfamilias's Mulholland Drive home on May 16, 1990. Santa Monica Superior Court Judge Robert Thomas imposed the sentence on Christian Brando to end the circus hearings, which included an hour of testimony from his famous father. Accepting a conviction on a voluntary manslaughter charge to escape a murder trial, Christian maintained he was trying to help Cheyenne extricate herself from her relationship with Drollet. Christian, who copped to anger issues, served six years at the California Men's Colony at San Luis Obispo and then was released. He married Deborah Presley, who unsuccessfully tried to prove she was Elvis's daughter out of wedlock. Brando's son and Elvis's maybe-daughter didn't prove to be Ozzie and Harriet: Christian admitted to spousal abuse in 2005 and then died of pneumonia on January 26, 2008. He was forty-nine.

MARCH 1

1985—LIZA ON THE ROCKS

Liza Minnelli entered an undisclosed midwestern addiction center on this date, the Associated Press reported, to bolster the booze and tranquilizer antidotes she had received during seven weeks the previous year in the Betty Ford Center, the famous dry-out tank in Rancho Mirage, California. Her career slide continued with *Rent-a-Cop* (1987), *Arthur 2: On the Rocks* (1988) and *Stepping Out* (1991). Despite an up-and-down showbiz career, Liza remains one of only five women to win an Oscar, Tony, Emmy and Grammy (along with Helen Hayes, Audrey Hepburn, Rita Moreno and Whoopi Goldberg). Subsequent reports have indicated that she fell off the wagon occasionally, and not just during her bitter 2007 divorce from David Gest. She collapsed on stage in Sweden in 2007 and broke a leg tripping over her dog in 2011.

MARCH 2

For generations, Harry Cohn dictatorially ran Columbia Pictures. Once bankrolled by racketeers, Harry was as cruel and profane as they come, hated yet admired by such employees as Rita Hayworth and Glenn Ford, Ben Hecht and Frank Capra. Stories about studio vulgarians invariably were about Harry Cohn. Built out of Poverty Row, Columbia still made five Oscar-winning best pictures during Harry's reign of terror, including *From Here to Eternity* (1953), *On the Waterfront* (1954) and *The Bridge on the River Kwai* (1957). Cohn's funeral, held on this day on the Columbia lot, drew two thousand people, including Clifford Odets, who wrote the eulogy, and Danny Kaye, who delivered it. "Well," said Red Skelton, surveying the mourners, "it only proves what they say—give the public something they want to see and they'll come out for it."

MARCH 3

1960—HONEY! I'M NEVER COMING HOME!

The most beloved couple on American television in the 1950s (counting *Ozzie & Harriet*), movie star Lucille Ball and bandleader Desi Arnaz had put up a happy front on both *I Love Lucy* and in an untenable marriage. But Lucy finally maintained that their real and TV lives had been anything but funny or happy for years. In fact, her divorce papers, filed on this date, claimed that her twenty-year union with the Cuban bandleader had become a "nightmare." U.S. households reacted like Fred and Ethel Mertz: complete shock. Lucy suspected the sause-tilting Desi of being unfaithful. They untangled the knot that tied

them both to Desilu Productions with the matrimonial knot. In 1963, she bought out his half of what had once been Howard Hughes's RKO Radio Pictures and became the first woman in Hollywood history to run a studio solo. She sold it to Paramount's parent company, Gulf & Western, in 1967 for $17 million.

MARCH 4

1975—QUEEN KNIGHTS TRAMP

An English native, Charlie Chaplin, eighty-five, was wheeled on this date into the ornate ballroom of Buckingham Palace, where Queen Elizabeth II tapped him on both shoulders with a ceremonial sword and dubbed him Sir Charles, a knight commander of the British Empire. Chaplin perfunctorily announced that he was "getting drunk." To FBI director J. Edgar Hoover, who had worked to deport Chaplin for decades (and succeeded in disallowing him reentry to the United States in 1952), the honor would have been a travesty, the misplaced celebration of a Communist, indiscriminate philanderer and scoundrel. In 1944, Chaplin was acquitted of violating the Mann Act—transporting someone across state lines for immoral purposes—for paying the 1942 train fare from Hollywood to New York of former contract actress Joan Barry. Chaplin died on Christmas 1977 at his home in Switzerland. He was eighty-eight.

MARCH 5

1982—JOHN BELUSHI'S SPEEDBALL EXIT

The portly and outsized talent of the Not Ready for Primetime Players, John Belushi quickly rose from *Saturday Night Live!* to movie star in *National Lampoon's Animal House* (1978) and *The Blues Brothers* (1980). His sudden death on this date in the Chateau Marmont Hotel on Sunset Strip was attributable to an overdose combo of heroin and cocaine, known as a "speedball." He had spent the night in the company of Robert De Niro and Robin Williams at different points, but both were gone when the lethal overdose was administered by Catherine Evelyn Smith, a Canadian junkie and drug dealer. She sold her story of Belushi's death to the *National Enquirer*, and it appeared under the headline "I Killed John Belushi" on June 29, 1982. California authorities extradited Smith from Toronto and charged her with murder. The charge was plea-bargained to involuntary manslaughter. She served fifteen months in prison. Belushi was thirty-three.

MARCH 6

1967—EDDY WARBLES HIS LAST

Nelson Eddy was one of the most well-known baritones of his day, singing in operas, for recordings and in nightclubs, one of which—the Sans Souci Hotel in Palm Beach, Florida—heard his swan song on March 5, 1967. Eddy keeled over from a stroke as one of the most notable performers to collapse onstage and then die. Eddy's greatest fame was as a "light leading man" in nineteen musical films, most famously in eight lavish MGM productions opposite Jeanette MacDonald, including *Naughty Marietta* (1935), *Rose Marie* (1936) and *Sweethearts* (1938). Eddy suffered a cerebral hemorrhage as he performed with singing partner Gale Sherwood and accompanist Ted Paxson. He died in the wee hours of this date at age sixty-five.

MARCH 7

Charlie Sheen, the star of Oliver Stone's *Platoon* (1986) and *Wall Street* (1987) and other films, became the highest paid actor on television in the CBS-TV sitcom *Two and a Half Men*, earning $40 million from May 2010 to May 2011. When Sheen blamed producer Chuck Lorre for delaying production, Lorre's public response about his maverick star—an admitted drug abuser and whoremonger— was, "If Charlie Sheen outlives me, I'm really going to be pissed." Sheen challenged the producer to a fight, demanding a raise to $3 million per episode, and identified himself in the aftermath as a "bitchin', total frickin' rock star from Mars" on NBC's *Today Show*. The battle royal shut the sitcom down for the season. Sheen was fired, won a $25 million settlement and continues to receive residuals from *Two and a Half Men* syndication airings. He was replaced by Ashton Kutcher.

MARCH 8

2004—TAKING A POWDER

Robert Pastorelli was one of the more ubiquitous character actors of his day, enlivening such big films as *Beverly Hills Cop II* (1987), *Dances with Wolves* (1990), *Striking Distance* (1993) and *Eraser* (1996). He played a recurring role on the popular Candice Bergen sitcom *Murphy Brown*. There was nothing lively about him on this date: his corpse was found in his Hollywood Hills home. A syringe, spoon and white powder were near the body. Police had just reopened an investigation into the March 1999 shooting death of Pastorelli's then-girlfriend, Charemon Jonovich. Pastorelli was considered by police a person of interest in the initial investigation, which determined that her death was accidental. After Pastorelli's death, Jonovich's death certificate was changed to record her exit as a homicide. The Los Angeles County coroner reported that Pastorelli died of "acute cocaine-morphine toxicity." He was forty-nine. Jonovich was twenty-five.

MARCH 9

1996—BURNS DENIES ODDSMAKERS

George Burns, who was born Naftaly Birnbaum on January 20, 1896, in New York City, confounded dead-pool wagering for more than a generation when he finally kicked the bucket on this date, a month and change past his 100th birthday. He died of a heart attack in Beverly Hills. The cigar-brandishing veteran of all entertainment media proved them wrong so often that his very mortality

was questioned. He was already at the half-century mark during the Truman administration and expired nine presidents later on Bill Clinton's watch. A wisecrack attributable to Dean Martin was, "When George was growing up, the top ten were the Ten Commandments." Burns was fond of recalling vaudeville, when Altoona, Pennsylvania, was a big gig. He won the Oscar for best supporting actor in *The Sunshine Boys* (1975) and perhaps had put in a celestial request to avoid the grim reaper as the title star of *Oh, God!* (1977) and its sequels.

MARCH 10

2010—A TEEN STAR'S CAREER

Corey Haim's "A" pictures—*Murphy's Romance* (1986), *The Lost Boys* (1987)—dipped by the 1990s with his drug habit to straight-to-video junk: *Snowboard Academy* (1996), *Demolition University* (1997). He was sued by Lloyd's of London in 1996 for $375,000 after being fired from *Paradise Bar* for failing to disclose addictions. He filed for bankruptcy. His assets were $100 in cash, $7,500 in royalties and residuals and a ten-year-old BMW. Haim recovered from a 2001 stroke and coma attributable to drugs. His auctioning of his hair and molars on the Internet was shut down by eBay's rule against selling body parts. In 2007, Haim and pal Corey Feldman starred in their own reality series, *The Two Coreys*. Both Feldman and Haim's girlfriend, Nicole Eggert, have claimed that Haim was sexually molested throughout his boyhood. A fifteen-time vet of rehab tango, Haim died on this date of natural causes, according to the Los Angeles County coroner. He was thirty-eight.

MARCH 11

1931—MURNAU DIES YOUNG

The great German filmmaker F.W. Murnau—*Nosferatu* (1922), *Faust* (1926)—made his masterpiece, *Sunrise* (1927), in America, followed by *Tabu* (1931), a South Seas epic. Its premiere was a week away when Murnau decided on a West Coast road trip in a Packard driven by his fourteen-year-old Filipino valet, Garcia Stevenson. The car collided with a truck near Santa Barbara on the Coast Highway and Stevenson was killed, while the director expired from a fractured skull a few hours later in a Santa Barbara hospital. *Tabu*, shot on Bora Bora, was censored in the United States for its depiction of bare-breasted Polynesian girls; however, cinematographer Floyd Crosby won the Oscar for his work. Murnau was portrayed by John Malkovich in a fictionalized account of the making of the film *Nosferatu*, called *Shadow of the Vampire* (2000), in which he hires an actual vampire named Max Schreck (Willem Dafoe) to star in the film. Murnau was forty-two.

MARCH 12

1978—GONE TOO QUICKLY

John Cazale was one of the luckiest actors, project-wise, in motion picture history. Longevity-wise, he wasn't so good. A lanky presence with a faraway stare and a mop of straight hair hanging back from a receding hairline, Cazale costarred in five movies—*every single one* a nominee for the best picture Oscar. In picking projects or them picking him, he batted 1.000 with three by director Francis Ford Coppola—*The Godfather* (1972), *The Conversation* (1974) and *The Godfather Part II* (1974)—as well as Sidney Lumet's *Dog Day Afternoon* (1975) and Michael Cimino's *The Deer Hunter* (1978). The first, third and final ones on the list won the best picture Oscar. When footage of him from the first two *Godfather* films was reprised in Coppola's *The Godfather Part III* (1990), that one was nominated for best picture as well. Cazale also costarred in three with Al Pacino, two with Robert De Niro and in *The Deer Hunter* with his paramour, Meryl Streep, even as he was dying from terminal lung cancer. He died on this date at age forty-two.

MARCH 13

1947—THE MAD AND THE BEAUTIFUL

Fashion designer Oleg Cassini married the shapely Gene Tierney in 1941. Studio boss Darryl F. Zanuck once said she was "undeniably the most beautiful woman in movie history." But the Cassinis couldn't manage her increasing mental illness, even as she graced some of Hollywood's finest films: *Heaven Can Wait* (1943), *Laura* (1944) and *The Razor's Edge* (1946). Their uncontested divorce occurred on this date. Her romance with young U.S. Navy officer John F. Kennedy was curtailed by his political ambitions. Gene quit movies for seven years and then for good after *The Pleasure Seekers* (1964) and married Texas oil tycoon W. Howard Lee in 1960—after he divorced Hedy Lamarr. Candid about her illness in her autobiography, *Self-Portrait* (1979), Tierney died in 1991 of emphysema in Houston, Texas. She was seventy.

MARCH 14

2008—Docs Exonerated

Five years after the death of John Ritter, a radiologist and cardiologist were found not responsible for the actor's death on this date by a Los Angeles County Superior Court jury. Ritter's family had already received $14 million in settlements, including $9.4 million from Providence St. Joseph Medical Center in Burbank, where he died on September 11, 2003, after falling ill during rehearsals on the sitcom *8 Simple Rules for Dating My Teenage Daughter*. The star of the sitcom *Three's Company* from 1976 to 1984, Ritter died from an aortic dissection caused by a previously undiagnosed congenital heart defect. His father, the famous recording star and cowboy actor Tex Ritter, had died of a heart attack nearly three decades earlier, at age sixty-eight. His mother, actress Dorothy Fay, died two months after John of natural causes. Ritter's wife, actress Amy Yasbeck, who costarred with him in *Problem Child* (1990), filed the original $67 million suit against the medicos. John Ritter was fifty-four, Dorothy eighty-eight.

MARCH 15

Arthur Richard Jackson, an itinerant Scot, stabbed Theresa Saldana on this date after stalking her through a private eye and posing as director Martin Scorsese's assistant. Jackson used the ruse of Scorsese possibly hiring the actress for another movie role; she had been featured in the director's *Raging Bull* (1980). In front of Saldana's West Hollywood residence, Jackson stabbed the costar of *The Evil That Men Do* (1984), *Of Men and Angels* (1989) and other films ten times. He bent the blade on her. Jeff Fenn heard the screams and rushed from a nearby building to disarm Jackson. Saldana recovered after a four-month stay at the Motion Picture Country Home & Hospital in Woodland Hills, California. She relived the incident for the made-for-TV movie *Victim for Victims: The Theresa Saldana Story* (1984). Jackson served a fourteen-year prison term and was extradited to the UK in 1996 to be tried for another murder. He died in prison in 2004. Fenn became a Los Angeles County deputy sheriff. Saldana remains an activist for victims' rights.

MARCH 16

Will Rogers presented the Academy Awards as master of ceremonies at the Ambassador Hotel in Los Angeles on this date, and as the multidimensional movie star, syndicated columnist and radio personality opened the envelope for best director of 1932/1933, he announced simply, "Come up and get it, Frank!" The director of *Lady for a Day*, Frank Capra, ran to the podium. But Rogers actually was beckoning Frank Lloyd, director of *Cavalcade*, the eventual best picture winner. It was Lloyd who won the best director statuette. So with two directors on stage named Frank, and to cover his gaffe, Rogers implored George Cukor, the other of the three total nominees for best director, for *Little Women*, to come up and join them, which Cukor did. Capra only had to wait a year to get his best director Oscar, for *It Happened One Night* (1934).

MARCH 17

1972—*PINK FLAMINGOS* RELEASED

John Waters's films are an acquired tastelessness or, in the director's mission to make trash acceptable, an acquired trashiness. They hit the fan in a big way on this date with the first national release of a Waters film, *Pink Flamingos*, which the writer, producer, composer, cinematographer, editor and director made on weekends in Phoenix, a Baltimore suburb. The film's depiction of flamboyant drag queen actor Divine eating dog crap is its most infamous moment. Produced for $10,000 and distributed by New Line Cinema, the film poses Divine as criminal mastermind Babs Johnson living the trailer-park life with her son, Crackers, and mentally deficient mother, Edie. A tabloid names Babs "the filthiest person alive," infuriating rival couple Connie and Raymond Marble. Waters went on to direct *Female Trouble* (1974), *Polyester* (1981), *Hairspray* (1988), *Cry-Baby* (1990), *Serial Mom* (1994) and others.

MARCH 18

The daughter of Oscar-winning actress Vanessa Redgrave and Oscar-winning director Tony Richardson, Natasha Richardson was the grandchild of Sir Michael Redgrave and Rachel Kempson, niece of Lynn and Corin Redgrave and wife of Liam Neeson. Natasha's films included *Patty Hearst* (1988), *The Comfort of Strangers* (1990) and *Nell* (1994). Natasha fell during a skiing lesson on March 16, 2009, at Mont Tremblant Resort in Quebec, Canada. Refusing medical attention at the site, she complained later of a headache. Stays in local and Montreal hospitals were followed by a flight in critical condition to Lenox Hill Hospital in New York City, where she died on this date. The New York City medical examiner determined that the accidental cause of death was epidural hematoma due to blunt impact to the head. On March 19, theater lights were dimmed in remembrance of Natasha on Broadway and in London's West End. She was forty-five.

MARCH 19

1953—GREATEST SHAM ON EARTH

Cecil B. De Mille's cornball extravaganza of a waning way of entertainment life, *The Greatest Show on Earth*, a fictional melodrama following the Ringling Brothers, Barnum & Bailey Circus, won the Oscar for best picture of 1952 on this night over a field including John Ford's *The Quiet Man*, John Huston's *Moulin Rouge* and Fred Zinnemann's *High Noon*. This rivals the 1941 party, when Ford's *How Green Was My Valley* beat out Orson Welles's *Citizen Kane* as the most undeserving best picture winner. Starring Charlton Heston, Betty Hutton and James Stewart, *The Greatest Show on Earth* lurches with scenery-chewing Heston from one backstage melodrama to the next, reestablishing for a new generation the time-honored showbiz dilemmas of acrobats and clowns, little people and animal trainers, leaving no clichéd stone unturned.

MARCH 20

1992—SHARON'S BASIC INSTINCT

The former Miss Crawford County, Pennsylvania, Sharon Stone became one of Hollywood's bigger stars with the release on this date of *Basic Instinct*, about an investigation into serial killings. Stone's bisexual character, Catherine Tramell, was the main suspect. The most notorious scene in director Paul Verhoeven's film occurs when Catherine crosses and uncrosses her legs during interrogation, revealing that the actress was, in locker-room parlance, "going commando." Stone said she agreed to film the bush-flash scene with no panties but was unaware how explicit it would be onscreen. "I did not think that you would see my vagina in the scene," she later complained. "Later, when I saw it in the screening I was shocked." Verhoeven said, "As much as I love her, I hate her, too, especially after the lies she told the press about the shot between her legs." Screenwriter Joe Eszterhas claimed in his autobiography, *Hollywood Animal*, that Stone was well aware of the nudity required.

MARCH 21

1988—Comeuppance for a Shyster

Jerome Rosenthal represented Van Johnson, Gordon MacRae and Marie Windsor. He sued Hedy Lamarr, Joan Fontaine and Betty Grable. Jerry squandered all of Doris Day's and Dorothy Dandridge's money on bad investments. He represented Esperanza "Chata" Wayne, in her 1954 divorce from John Wayne, maintaining that the Duke should shell out "ma-in-law" payments—monthly $650 stipends to Chata's mom on top of alimony. An urban legend holds that the only understanding of justice this bilker-to-the-stars ever received came when the Duke filled his lunch order in the parking lot of Chasen's with a knuckle sandwich. "I'm reliably informed that Wayne did, however, have occasion to slug Jerry," wrote journalist Roger M. Grace, Jerry's one-time nephew-in-law. Jerry was disbarred by a unanimous vote of the U.S. Supreme Court on this date after the California Supreme Court affirmed bar findings that Rosenthal engaged in thirteen acts of misconduct, including conflicts of interest, double-billing, filing fraudulent claims, falsely testifying, harassing clients, obstructing justice, etc. Jerry died in 2007. He was ninety-six.

MARCH 22

1999—KAZAN'S SUCCINCT SPEECH

Elia Kazan won Oscars for directing the Oscar-winning best pictures *Gentleman's Agreement* (1947) and *On the Waterfront* (1954) and was nominated on five other occasions. On this night, at age eighty-nine, he received an honorary Oscar for his influence on theater and film acting. He brought the best out of Marlon Brando, James Dean, Natalie Wood, Montgomery Clift, Eva Marie Saint, Lee Remick, Warren Beatty and others. But his black mark suddenly loomed large: Kazan was characterized a stool pigeon when, in 1952, he named names before the House Un-American Activities Committee investigating Communist influences in Hollywood. The pro-con debate over his honorary Oscar electrified Hollywood for weeks. On Oscar night, Robert De Niro, who had starred in Kazan's *The Last Tycoon* (1976), said, "He was the master of a new kind of psychological and behavioral truth in acting...he...brought a thrilling new reality to the stage and screen." Kazan, deflecting any animosity, walked out, accepted the statuette, said, "Thank you," and walked off.

MARCH 23

1951—JUDY AND VINCENTE CALL IT QUITS

Judy Garland and director Vincente Minnelli met on the set of *Strike Up the Band* (1940), a Busby Berkeley musical for which Minnelli designed a sequence performed by the actress and Mickey Rooney. Garland and Minnelli began dating after resolving creative conflicts on the set of *Meet Me in St. Louis* (1944). They married in June 1945, and Liza Minnelli was born on March 12, 1946. On this date, Judy and Vincente were divorced, with her increasingly erratic behavior and narcotics use an issue, causing MGM to drop her contract in 1950. The jury is still out on the legend of Minnelli's supposedly gay lifestyle. The four-foot eleven-inch, howitzer-voiced Judy married producer Sid Luft on June 29, 1952. But the core Minnelli family remains singular in Hollywood history in that the father, mother and child all won Oscars: Vincenti won as best director for *Gigi* (1958); Judy won a special "juvenile" Oscar for the 1939 films *The Wizard of Oz* and *Babes in Arms*, and Liza captured the best actress statuette for *Cabaret* (1972).

MARCH 24

1962—JFK Snubs Frank

When John F. Kennedy campaigned for president, fellow Catholic Francis Albert Sinatra used his influence to help elect the Massachusetts silver spoon. When Frank learned that JFK was to visit his own adopted hometown of Palm Springs in 1962, the saloon singer responded with largess—bought extra land, built an extra guest house, installed amenities for the Secret Service and entourage, put in a new telephone system and a helicopter pad. On short notice, JFK instead stayed at Bing Crosby's Palm Springs mansion, ensconced with one of Frank's most incendiary old flames, Marilyn Monroe, or so some versions go. To put it mildly, Frank went nuts. He banished JFK's brother-in-law, Peter Lawford, from the Rat Pack for years because Lawford had been the go-between who promised to deliver the prez to Frank. In an epic snit, Sinatra went to work on the new quarters—with an axe and sledgehammer.

MARCH 25

2005—THE PITTS DIVORCE

It was a marriage made in *People* magazine heaven: sensible, saucy favorite Jennifer Aniston and the hideously handsome and talented Brad Pitt—until this date. And it was a marriage imploded through *People*'s pages, harkening back to an era when Hollywood royalty and the studios used press releases to manipulate the media. On January 7, 2005, Aniston and Pitt released a joint statement to *People*, which said: "We would like to announce that after seven years together we have decided to formally separate. For those who follow these sorts of things, we would like to explain that our separation is not the result of any of the speculation reported by the tabloid media. This decision is the result of much thoughtful consideration." Pitt, forty-one at the split, met Aniston, thirty-six at so-long, when they were set up on a dinner date in 1998. The pair had wed in Malibu on July 29, 2000.

MARCH 26

2002—JIM BROWN IN THE SLAMMER

Pro Football Hall of Fame running back and the star of such prison films as *The Dirty Dozen* (1967), *Riot* (1968) and *The Slams* (1973), Jim Brown, sixty-six, should have been very hungry on this date. In the second week of a hunger strike at the Ventura County Jail, he told the *New York Times*, "I'm fasting—I'm on a spiritual fast. That way I am setting the terms of my imprisonment." He was sentenced to six months on January 5, 2000, for a 1999 misdemeanor vandalism conviction that demonstrated a novel use for a shovel—smashing out the windows of his wife's Honda Accord. Judge Dale S. Fischer originally sentenced the former Cleveland Browns star to a year of domestic violence counseling. She had also ordered him to spend forty days on a work crew or four hundred hours of community service, pay $1,800 in fines and serve three years' probation. Brown refused the counseling. Five times Brown has been accused of threatening or attacking women, once in 1968, when he was accused of throwing Eva Marie Bohn-Chin, a German model, off a second-story balcony. Brown insists she jumped. Brown was released from his shovel-incident sentence after serving nearly four months of his six-month term on July 4, 2002.

MARCH 27

1973—SACHEEN LITTLEFEATHER

Marlon Brando was named the winner of the best actor Oscar for *The Godfather* (1972) on this date. Stepping to the podium on the actor's behalf was a tall Native American activist in Apache dress. She presented a brief speech while Brando boycotted the forty-fifth Academy Awards in protest of the treatment of Native Americans by the movie industry. The American Indian Movement (AIM) sent along Sacheen Littlefeather, but the producer backstage refused to let her read Brando's fifteen-page statement and gave her just sixty seconds. She improvised a few main points. She then went backstage and read the entire speech to the assembled press. In his autobiography, *My Word Is My Bond*, Roger Moore, who presented the award, says he took the Oscar home with him and kept it until it was collected by an armed guard sent by the Academy.

MARCH 28

1956—"RKO RADIOACTIVE PICTURE"

The Conqueror, starring John Wayne as Genghis Khan, was released by RKO Radio Pictures on this date. The shock in seeing the Duke as the thirteenth-century Mongol warlord couldn't have been more intense had the rugged icon tried Joan of Arc. The film was shot near St. George, Utah, 137 miles downwind from the U.S. government's Nevada Test Site for 1953 nuclear blasts. The real tragedy was much more far-reaching than miscasting: of the 220-member cast and crew, who had worked on location for weeks, 91 developed cancer by 1981, and 46 died from the disease. Director Dick Powell succumbed in 1963; costar Pedro Armendáriz the same year from a self-inflicted gunshot wound after he learned his case was terminal; stars Wayne, Susan Hayward and Agnes Moorehead in the 1970s; and John Hoyt in 1991. The connection between nuclear fallout and cancer remains unproven.

MARCH 29

Getting it wrong on Oscar night is an occasional tradition. The gaffe on this night was practiced. The sixty-first Academy Awards' opening number consisted of a sprawling Broadway-style version of Creedence Clearwater Revival's "Proud Mary," performed by actress Eileen Bowman, dressed as Snow White, with Rob Lowe under the gaze of Merv Griffin. Get a clip: Snow White, Rob Lowe, Merv and CCR. The Walt Disney Company considered a lawsuit for defamation of the Snow White character but dropped the idea. A wall-to-wall hiss hit producer Allan Carr like a gale, and he never guided the Oscars again. Bowman went on to appear in *Killer Tomatoes Eat France* (1992). Lowe segued into his Atlanta sex-tape scandal. Merv settled a 1991 lawsuit out of court by Deney Terrio, charging the daytime TV demagogue with sexual harassment while the latter was host of *Dance Fever*. And Oscar continued on.

MARCH 30

1968—DRISCOLL IN POTTER'S FIELD

A well-regarded child actor of his generation, Bobby Driscoll starred in *Song of the South* (1946), *The Window* (1949), *Treasure Island* (1950) and others. His roles dwindled with age, and trouble followed: disturbing the peace, assault with a deadly weapon, drug possession. In 1961, he was remanded to the California Institution for Men at Chino. He drifted from an unkind Broadway into Andy Warhol's Greenwich Village artists' enclave, "The Factory." Driscoll's last performance was in the underground film *Dirt* (1965), the subject of which soon covered him. On this date, about three weeks after his thirty-first birthday, Bobby's body was found in a tenement. The medical examination determined heart failure related to longtime narcotics abuse. Driscoll's unclaimed body was buried in Potter's Field on Hart Island in western Long Island Sound. Nineteen months after his death, Driscoll's mother hoped to reunite Bobby with his father, who was near death. This resulted in an NYPD fingerprint match with the Potter's Field corpse.

MARCH 31

1993—Brandon Lee Shot and Killed

While acting a scene in *The Crow* in Wilmington, North Carolina, on this date, Brandon Lee entered his character's loft to discover his fiancée being raped. Actor Michael Massee, in character, fired a revolver at Lee, who immediately collapsed. When Lee failed to get up, the cast and crew found that he was wounded. The second unit, running late, had made dummy cartridges—functional ammo with no propellant or primers—from real cartridges by pulling out the bullets and dumping the propellant. Unknown to anyone, a bullet was lodged in the barrel. When the first blank cartridge was fired, the force of the primer, though not close to the bullet, was able to propel it out of the gun and into Lee's abdomen. It lodged near his spine. Lee was rushed to the New Hanover Regional Medical Center. After a six-hour operation, he was pronounced dead. He was twenty-eight.

APRIL 1

1998—MOUSE EARS ON AN EGGHEAD HOAX

The wonderful world of Disney was apparently getting an injection of intellect on this date: MIT was coming to the rescue. Goofy would get a slide rule, Herbie GPS and Tinkerbell a laser wand. The homepage of the Massachusetts Institute of Technology announced the startling news: the prestigious Cambridge, Massachusetts university was to be sold to the Walt Disney Company for $6.9 billion. A photograph of MIT's landmark dome sporting mouse ears accompanied the news. The press release on the site explained that the university was to be dismantled, transported to Orlando, Florida, and reassembled. New courses would include the Scrooge McDuck School of Management and the Donald Duck Department of Linguistics. Computer geeks actually had hacked into the school's central server and put up the bogus announcement. April Fools!

APRIL 2

At the forty-sixth Academy Awards ceremony, a streaker named Robert Opel ran across the stage naked while flashing the peace sign behind host David Niven at the podium. "Isn't it fascinating to think that the only laugh that man will ever get in his life is by stripping…and showing his shortcomings?" Niven quipped. Opel had been a photojournalist and was able to get a backstage pass. In retrospect, Robert Metzler, the show's business manager, believed the stunt was planned by Niven and the producer, Jack Haley Jr. In 2001, this full-frontal moment was voted the most memorable in Oscar history. Four years after his Oscar streak, Opel opened Fey-Way Studios, a gallery of gay male art, on Howard Street in San Francisco. On July 7, 1979, during a robbery by drug dealers at the studio, Opel was murdered by being shot in the head.

APRIL 3

1978—HOODLUMS-SCHMOODLUMS

The use of Oscar's worldwide podium to espouse causes other than the art and science of motion pictures saw perhaps its most strident speech in that vein when Vanessa Redgrave won the Oscar for best supporting actress on this night as the title character in *Julia*. The most celebrated Redgrave used the opportunity to comment about "Zionist hoodlums," bringing scattered boos and some applause. Paddy Chayefsky, who wrote the Oscar-winning screenplays for *Marty* (1955), *The Hospital* (1971) and *Network* (1976), prefaced his presentations of the screenwriting awards later in the telecast by saying he was tired of people exploiting the Oscars "for the propagation of their own personal political propaganda." Chayefsky said, "I would like to suggest to Miss Redgrave that her winning an Academy Award is not a pivotal moment in history, does not require a proclamation, and a mere thank you would have sufficed." Thank *you*.

APRIL 4

1958—LANA COULD REALLY PICK 'EM

Johnny Stompanato, the infamously jealous boyfriend of Lana Turner, the glamorous star of *The Postman Always Rings Twice* (1946), *The Bad and the Beautiful* (1952) and *Peyton Place* (1957), was better known by aliases: "Johnny Stomp," aka "Oscar," aka "Handsome Harry," aka "John Steele." One of LA rackets kingpin Mickey Cohen's bodyguards, the stocky ex-marine wore lizard-skin shoes and threw his weight around, like on this night, and right at Lana. Her daughter, Cheryl Crane, retaliated by stabbing the gangster in the kidney and the aorta. Johnny Stomp had survived war's ravages at Peleliu and Okinawa only to bleed to death from a teen girl's stab on the floor of Lana Turner's Beverly Hills mansion. The courts ruled the death a justifiable homicide—Cheryl was protecting her mom, who went on to her fifth, sixth and seventh marriages. Earlier hubbies included Artie Shaw and one of Hollywood's Tarzans, Lex Barker, whom Crane accused of sexually assaulting her in her 1988 autobiography, *Detour: A Hollywood Tragedy*, in which she also detailed the story of Johnny Stomp. He was thirty-two.

Kirk Douglas and Lana Turner personified movie-industry folks in Vincente Minnelli's *The Bad and the Beautiful* (1952).

APRIL 5

1976—HOWARD HUGHES DIES HIGH

Billionaire recluse Howard Hughes, all six feet, four inches of him at ninety pounds, self-medicated beyond sense, with hair down his back and fingernails as long as a raptor's talons, was allegedly completely unrecognizable when he ceased living on this date. The end for the aviation pioneer came appropriately in the air, aboard his private plane en route from Acapulco, Mexico, to Houston, Texas. The corpse, admitted to Houston's Methodist Hospital under Hughes's longtime alias, "John T. Conover," was identified by FBI fingerprints. The cause of death was kidney failure exacerbated by malnutrition. Five broken-off hypodermic needles were found in his arms. Six months after becoming the first sole boss of a Hollywood movie studio in three decades in 1954, he sold RKO Radio Pictures in 1955 for $25 million to General Tire & Rubber Company of Akron, Ohio, ending his Hollywood career. One of America's most fascinating eccentrics was seventy.

APRIL 6

1997—FRANK: YOU'RE THROUGH IN THIS TOWN

James Farentino's three years of probation for stalking Frank Sinatra's younger daughter, Tina Sinatra, ended this week along with his career. In the very industry that prompted the creation of the stalking laws, Farentino's dumbest move after his crimes was pestering the daughter of a guy who, even in his final stanzas, could summon piano movers with a finger snap. Emmy nominated as Simon Peter in *Jesus of Nazareth* (1976) and a star of *The Bold Ones*, *Dynasty* and other series and films, Farentino copped to twenty-four stalking-law violations on March 31, 1994, following his bust by Royal Canadian Mounted Police in 1991 in Vancouver for cocaine possession. Farentino's first wife, actress Elizabeth Ashley, defected to George Peppard, and the second, actress Michele Lee, aired their rocky relationship in *People* magazine in 1981. Jimmy dated Tina for five years before she told him that he was no longer a Sinatra costar. He died from complications of a broken hip on January 24, 2012, bitter over his blacklisting. He was seventy-three.

APRIL 7

After years of litigation, *Basic Instinct 2: Risk Addiction* was in its first week of release on this date, its fortunes tied to a sinking Stone—Sharon. The sequel to *Basic Instinct* (1992) had been made by director Michael Caton-Jones in the spring and summer of 2005 in London. Its delay was reportedly over Stone's dispute with the filmmakers over the nudity in the film. Unlike her complaints over the first film's level of nudity, this time she wanted more and they wanted less. A group sex scene was cut to achieve an R rating instead of the more restrictive NC-17 from the Motion Picture Association of America for the U.S. release. The controversial scene remained in the UK version. "We are in a time of odd repression and if a popcorn movie allows us to create a platform for discussion, wouldn't that be great?" Stone said. The $70 million MGM movie made $6 million in domestic earnings.

APRIL 8

1986—His Honor, Mayor Clint

When the polls closed on this date in Carmel-by-the-Sea, California, the tallies showed that, with twice the voter turnout than in the previous mayoral election, Clinton Eastwood Jr. won 72.5 percent of the vote. He was sworn in a week later in an inauguration ceremony that was absent firearms. Clint mended fences with incumbent mayor Charlotte Townsend by giving her a potted redwood seedling. The campaign motto for a guy famous for explaining the decapitating capability of a .357 Magnum was "Bring the Community Together." Clint approached the job of mayor the way he has with movie producing: with business acumen. The method in this Eastwood madness, which earned him $200 a month, was to clear the red tape out of city hall zoning and building permits. He became known for supporting small businesses and environmentalism. He shepherded the building of a children's library. No one in city hall was harmed during his mayoral term.

APRIL 9

2001—BLADE FRACAS AT THE FIREBELLY LOUNGE

One of America's most admired character actors, Steve Buscemi, was stabbed in the throat, head, arm and hands on this date in a barroom brawl that had spilled outside the Firebelly Lounge in Wilmington, North Carolina. Buscemi, Vince Vaughn and screenwriter Scott Rosenberg were slaking thirsts in the bar during a respite from filming *Domestic Disturbance*. Vaughn talked to the girlfriend of a patron—perceived as Hollywood types cutting in on the local action—inciting contretemps. The rumble moved outside, and Buscemi was cut. A gaunt, familiar, expressive-eyed presence in offbeat films, including *Reservoir Dogs* (1992), *Fargo* (1996) and *The Big Lebowski* (1998), Buscemi was hospitalized for his wounds and blood loss and then flown to New York. One Timothy Fogerty was charged with assault with a deadly weapon. Rosenberg, who wrote *Con Air* (1997) and *High Fidelity* (2000), and Vaughn, as well as two Wilmington men, were booked for misdemeanor assault. Charges were later dropped.

APRIL 10

1965—ASH TO ASH, STARDUST TO DUST

Linda Darnell was considered one of the screen's great beauties, starring in John Ford's *My Darling Clementine* (1946), Otto Preminger's *Forever Amber* (1947) and Joseph L. Mankiewicz's *A Letter to Three Wives* (1949). But by the 1960s, in her forties, she segued, as many former screen sirens did, into guest star roles on television. Linda returned to the stage and was staying with friends on this date in Glenview, Illinois, while preparing for a Chicago performance. Ronald L. Davis's biography, *Hollywood Beauty* (1991), claims no evidence exists that she was drunk, fell asleep with a lit cigarette or was despondent over her career decline. She was not responsible for the house fire that burned over 90 percent of her body. Her ashes are buried at the Union Hill Cemetery in Chester County, Pennsylvania. She was forty-one.

Linda Darnell and Paul Douglas costarred in Joseph L. Mankiewicz's *A Letter to Three Wives* (1949).

APRIL 11

2001—United States v. Snipes

On December 9, 2010, Wesley Snipes began serving a three-year term in the Federal Correctional Institution, McKean, in Allegheny National Forest in Pennsylvania. His 2008 conviction was for income tax evasion. On June 6, 2011, the U.S. Supreme Court declined to hear his appeal. The star of *White Men Can't Jump* (1992), *Blade* (1998), *One Night Stand* (1998) and other movies could have been sent up for felonies for filing fraudulent claims and conspiracy, but appellate courts upheld the lower court ruling. The original counts filed against him in 2006 in U.S. District Court in Orlando, Florida, included that Snipes and two pals knowingly filed a fraudulent claim on this date for the 1997 tax year for a refund to Snipes in the amount of $7,360,755. Snipes willfully did not file tax returns from 1999 through 2004. Snipes had been a client of American Rights Litigators, operated by Eddie Ray Kahn, who was sentenced to ten years on a felony conspiracy rap to defraud the United States.

APRIL 12

1914—FIRST MOVIE PALACE

The Mark Strand Theatre, first of the movie "dream palaces," opened to the public on this date at Broadway and 47th Street in New York City. It was designed by Mitchell H. Mark, a producer turned exhibitor. This bold marketing move brought the flickers to a wider audience, creating a moviegoing experience of comfort and luxury and helping to cast a spell over film addicts or further corrupt them, depending on the prevailing points of view. Prior to the Strand, "nickelodeons" operated behind various storefronts, named after the original Nickelodeon that opened in Pittsburgh in 1905. "The Strand" was cavernous in size, with graceful architectural features, seating for three thousand, a second-floor balcony and a two-story rotunda lobby. The opening-night movie was *The Spoilers*, starring William Farnum. Feature film production ramped up to fill the palaces, which numbered more than twenty thousand across the nation before 1920.

APRIL 13

Sidney Poitier became the first African American male actor on this date to win an Academy Award, playing a handyman who builds a Catholic chapel in *Lilies of the Field* (1963). A triumph for actors of color, or actors anywhere of uncommon talent, Poitier's victory was not exactly a popular occurrence in the racist corners of the American South in a year when civil rights campaigns turned into bloody skirmishes with the Ku Klux Klan. Also, Big Sid, playing an everyman in a quiet little film, had beat out Paul Newman in *Hud* and three Brits: Albert Finney, Richard Harris and Rex Harrison. Other black actors have since won the gold—Lou Gossett Jr., Denzel Washington, Morgan Freeman, Forest Whitaker—but Big Sid was the trailblazer. He never was nominated again, despite, in 1967, starring in three films showered with nominations: *Guess Who's Coming to Dinner*; *To Sir, with Love*; and best picture winner *In the Heat of the Night*.

APRIL 14

John Wayne donned an eye patch and a boozy, grumpy demeanor to play U.S. Marshal Rooster Cogburn in director Henry Hathaway's western *True Grit* (1969). The Duke satirized his own legend and invested Cogburn with ample amounts of irascibility, machismo and corn—all the way to the best actor Oscar. He edged out Dustin Hoffman and Jon Voight in best picture winner *Midnight Cowboy*, as well as Brits Richard Burton and Peter O'Toole. The win was unexpected in that considerations of Wayne as an anachronism were alive in a nation amid a youth-culture reinvigoration. The Duke had been persona non grata for foisting the jingoistic *The Green Berets* (1968) on a public worn out by the Vietnam War and protests against it. Accepting the Oscar from presenter Barbra Streisand, the Duke was humbled but also cracked that had he known he could have won an Oscar, he would have "put that eye patch on thirty-five years ago."

APRIL 15

Part of the overbearing grumpiness that inhabited George C. Scott's performance as General George S. Patton Jr. in his Oscar-winning role in *Patton* (1970) also informed the actor's real life. The raspy-voiced native of Wise, Virginia, refused the Oscar because he thought Academy Awards politicking was "demeaning" and the ceremony was "a two-hour meat parade." Scott made the role indelible, so it's difficult imagining director Franklin J. Schaffner's initial choices; he had offered it to Burt Lancaster, Robert Mitchum, Lee Marvin and Rod Steiger, all of whom turned it down. Schaffner staved off the pursuit of John Wayne, who badly wanted to play the legendary general, before Scott accepted. Scott and Marlon Brando, who refused his Academy Award a year later for *The Godfather* (1972), are the only two actors who refused their Oscars. Scott told the Academy of Motion Picture Arts & Sciences to give the Oscar to the General George Patton Museum in Fort Knox, Kentucky. Since the academy didn't receive a written directive, it has maintained possession of the statuette. Scott died in 1999 at age seventy-one.

APRIL 16

1981—HAYDEN: HASH AND CASH WOES

Sterling Hayden was arrested on this date at Toronto International Airport for hashish possession. A Canadian judge dismissed the charge after Hayden's lawyer said the actor used hash to battle alcoholism. Hayden, a rangy, baritone-voiced former sea captain, won the Silver Star as an OSS operative in Italy in World War II when his cobbled-together flotilla manned by partisans ran munitions through the German blockade of the Adriatic Sea to Tito's Communists fighting the Nazis in the Dinaric Alps. Hayden was one of the more ubiquitous stars of film noir—*The Asphalt Jungle* (1950), *Crime Wave* (1954), *The Killing* (1956)—but his most celebrated role was as General Jack D. Ripper, who launches World War III, in *Dr. Strangelove* (1964). The IRS sought the always-broke actor throughout his life, much of it spent in Europe on his Dutch barge. Steven Spielberg wanted the seaman as Captain Quint in *Jaws* (1975), but the feds would have nabbed him had he then returned to the United States. (Robert Shaw played the part.) Hayden died in 1986 in Sausalito, California. He was seventy.

Sterling Hayden starred with Jean Hagen in John Huston's heist caper *The Asphalt Jungle* (1950).

APRIL 17

The Oscar campaign in the trade papers *Variety* and *The Hollywood Reporter* for producer-director-star John Wayne's *The Alamo* (1960) was one of the most politicized of all time. But the Duke's overall campaigning was upstaged to some degree by fellow cast member Chill Wills, who played Beekeeper, Davy Crockett's booze-swilling buddy. Nominated for best supporting actor, Wills went all out. One ad read: "We of *The Alamo* cast are praying harder than the real Texans prayed for their lives at the Alamo for Chill Wills to win the Oscar." Wills characterized himself as a relative, signing ads, "Your Alamo cousin." Even the Duke was peeved at Wills's shamelessness. Groucho Marx wrote to a trade paper, "Dear Mr. Wills. I am delighted to be your cousin. But I'm voting for Sal Mineo." Peter Ustinov won the best supporting actor Oscar of 1960 for *Spartacus*.

APRIL 18

One of the more extemporaneous comics of his time, Dick Shawn had starred in *It's a Mad Mad Mad Mad World* (1963), *Way…Way Out* (1966), *The Producers* (1968) and *Love at First Bite* (1979), among many films, and was a frequent television, nightclub and campus-circuit performer. Audience members who saw him perform the evening before this date, onstage at UC–San Diego's Mandeville Hall, had their worst suspicions confirmed in the *San Diego Union*. After a few bits in which he mocked a politician who would never lay down on the job, Shawn collapsed face-down on the stage. After some time, catcalls ensued and a stagehand examined the horizontal comic, stood and asked, "Is there a doctor in the house?" CPR began, and the audience was told to go home, but few left immediately, some accustomed to Shawn's unconventional humor. However, he actually expired before their eyes of a heart attack. Shawn was sixty-three.

APRIL 19

Federico Fellini's *La Dolce Vita* (1960), a series of vignettes about the languid and promiscuous lives of upper-crust Romans, was released in the United States on this date. It brought the entrance of the scandal-handle "paparazzi" into the English language as an eponym for fame-magnetized, intrusive, exploitation "news" photographers. By the 1970s, the term was in general use. A character in the picture is a motor scooter–riding news photographer named Paparazzo, played by Walter Santesso. Fellini once said the name derived from Italian slang for an annoying noise—a mosquito's buzz. The English plural usage of the word *paparazzi* is traced to Italian poet Margherita Guidacci in her translation of George Gissing's travel book *By the Ionian Sea* (1901), in which a restaurant owner is named Coriolano Paparazzo. *La Dolce Vita* screenplay contributor Ennio Flaiano said Fellini supplied the name after opening Guidacci's *Sulla riva dello Jonio* (1957) at random.

APRIL 20

1968—Doris Day: Que Sera, Sera

Ever-perky Doris Day, known as the "world's oldest virgin" as mores changed in the late 1960s, was nevertheless Hollywood's most bankable actress early in the decade, opposite Rock Hudson in *Pillow Talk* (1959) and other films, Cary Grant in *That Touch of Mink* (1962) and James Garner in *Move Over, Darling* (1963). Day discovered she was broke on this date—after all those hits as well as successful recordings—when her husband, film producer Marty Melcher, died of what was thought to be a ruptured appendix. A practicing Christian Scientist, Marty eschewed medicine, deteriorated rapidly and died at fifty-two. Marty's business partner was bilker-to-the-stars Jerome Rosenthal, and he had squandered Day's millions. She immediately accepted a deal with CBS-TV for *The Doris Day Show*. In February 1969, she sued Rosenthal for her career earnings. On September 18, 1974, she won the $22.8 million suit, then the largest civil judgment in California history. Shyster Jerry tied up the payments until 1979, whittling them to $6 million.

APRIL 21

2005—"COS" FOR ALARM

Innovative stand-up comic, author of the bestselling *Fatherhood* (1987) and ten other books, movie star in *Hickey & Boggs* (1972), *Uptown Saturday Night* (1974) and other films and an immense television star with *I Spy*, *The Cosby Show* and other series, Bill Cosby has been one of the most influential and beloved icons of American entertainment. A figure of principle and thoughtfulness, "the Cos" has been conferred with the Kennedy Center Honor, Mark Twain Prize for American Humor, Presidential Medal of Freedom and a dozen honorary doctorates. In 2005, at age sixty-seven, Cosby also became the most infamous accused rapist in America. After a former Temple University employee, Andrea Constand, sued Cosby in March 2005 for allegedly drugging and raping her, she withdrew the suit after an assumed big payoff. However, ten other women accused the man who played Cliff Huxtable of similar crimes over several decades. Nine were cited as "Jane Doe" along with a Ventura County, California lawyer, Tamara Green. These unproven "prior bad acts" hit the media on this date, the day after they were filed in U.S. District Court in Philadelphia. The district attorney of Montgomery County, Pennsylvania, where Cosby lives, declined on April 22 to file criminal charges.

APRIL 22

Being the black sheep of the Baldwin brothers takes some effort. Daniel Baldwin was arrested on this date by Santa Monica police after they received a call that a woman had been threatened at the Ocean Park Motel. Police declined to press charges this time. The incident followed Daniel's more infamous February 2, 1998 arrest at the Plaza Hotel in New York, when police cuffed him for possession of cocaine and disorderly conduct after he roamed the halls buck naked shouting his surname: "Baldwin!…Baldwin!…" Following the motel imbroglio, on July 19, 2006, in West LA, Danny-boy, whose movies include *Hero* (1992) and *Mulholland Falls* (1996), plowed a rented Ford Thunderbird into a Hummer at eighty miles per hour. On November 7, 2007, Danny was arrested for stealing an SUV, but the charges were dropped. Twice more, arrest warrants were issued for the brother of Alec, Stephen and Billy Baldwin—both times for failure to appear in court. A rehab-tango vet, Danny costarred on *Celebrity Rehab with Dr. Drew* but left the show after it was disclosed that he sent inappropriate text messages to a fellow rehab group member, Mary Carey, a porn star.

APRIL 23

Albert Salmi was one of the television era's most familiar character actors, hitting high points as the dying catcher in the original TV production of *Bang the Drum Slowly* (1956) with Paul Newman and George Peppard and in director George C. Scott's Emmy-winning *The Andersonville Trial* (1970). A rangy Method actor with a powerful presence, often in westerns, Salmi's star rose opposite Kim Stanley in the famed 1955 Broadway production of William Inge's *Bus Stop*. His films include Elia Kazan's *Wild River* (1960), *Brubaker* (1980) and *Caddyshack* (1980). Writing his memoirs, Salmi allegedly became despondent over his separation from his wife, Roberta. On this date, police found the bodies of Albert and Roberta in his Spokane, Washington home. An apparent murder-suicide, the acts were committed with different guns. He was shot through the heart with a Colt .45. He was sixty-two. Roberta was fifty-five.

APRIL 24

During a baseball game on this date, the Pittsburgh Pirates' twenty-three-year veteran broadcaster, Lanny Frattare, reported the death of James Earl Jones and then reminisced about the cavern-voiced actor's role in *Field of Dreams*. Lanny said he "misunderstood" when his producer told him that Martin Luther King Jr.'s assassin, James Earl Ray, had died. For his gaffe, Frattare was named "Dweeb of the Week" by the *New York Daily News*. But mistaken deaths and death hoaxes are practically a pastime. In 1982, *People* magazine mistakenly referred to the "late Abe Vigoda," which the *Barney Miller* character actor used for years as shtick, including on *Late Night with David Letterman* when Dave tried summoning Abe's ghost; Vigoda appeared and told the host, "I'm not dead yet, you pinhead." In recent years, hoaxes or mistaken reports declared dead Russell Crowe, Jeff Goldblum, Adam Sandler, Natalie Portman, Jackie Chan, Madonna, Jaclyn Smith, Will Ferrell and Betty White.

APRIL 25

1972—"DEAR WORLD, I AM LEAVING..."

The droll and urbane George Sanders won his best supporting actor Oscar as the stage critic Addison De Witt in director Joseph L. Mankiewicz's *All About Eve* (1950). A know-it-all weariness informed many of Sanders's 150-plus performances, including his final one as himself. Sanders consumed five tubes of Nembutal at Castelldefels, near Barcelona, Spain, on this date, leaving behind one of the more cynical bye-bye notes of all time: "Dear World, I am leaving, because I am bored. I feel I have lived long enough. I am leaving you with your worries in this sweet cesspool. Good luck." Three of his four marriages ended in divorce, and there's nothing to suggest that his suicide had anything to do with two of them having been to Gabor sisters—Zsa Zsa from 1949 to 1954 and Magda from 1970 to 1971. Sanders was sixty-five. His cremated ashes were scattered in the English Channel.

APRIL 26

1989—PALIMONY V. CLINT

While Sondra Locke was directing *Impulse* (1989), her longtime lover, Clint Eastwood, had the locks changed on their Bel Air house and moved many of her possessions to storage. Sondra fainted on the film's set after she received a phone call from her husband, Gordon Anderson. Gordon read a letter to her over the phone that had been left on his doorstep, stating that she was being evicted from her home and that Eastwood was giving her one month to get her belongings out of storage. She sued Clint for palimony on this date. Anderson, a gay sculptor, married Locke when she was twenty-three for both of their conveniences. The legal tangle was ostensibly settled when Clint agreed to get her a directing contract with Warner Bros., and then it was settled for an undisclosed sum after she legally complained that the contract was a sham. She dished the dirt with her autobiography, *The Good, the Bad, and the Very Ugly* (1997).

APRIL 27

1991—TEFLON BOB EVANS SKATES

As the head of Paramount Pictures and as the producer of such classics as *The Godfather* (1972), *The Godfather Part II* (1974) and *Chinatown* (1974), Robert Evans was a wheeler-dealer's wheeler-dealer. On this date, testimony exonerated him in a deal gone sour—and then deadly. One of his former lovers testified that he was not involved in the murder of New York theatrical producer Roy Radin in the infamous "*Cotton Club* case." Karen Delayne "Laynie" Greenberger, who was eventually convicted in the 1983 murder, also told jurors she believed her own life had been saved on the night Radin was slain. It turned out she believed that she was being squeezed out of a producer's credit on the Francis Ford Coppola–directed *The Cotton Club* (1984) and was convicted for conspiring with three others to bump off Radin. She was sentenced to life in prison without the possibility of parole in 1992. Evans went on to produce *The Two Jakes* (1990) and *Jade* (1995) and write his memoirs, *The Kid Stays in the Picture*.

APRIL 28

2011—"VIOLENT TORPEDO OF TRUTH"

Charlie Sheen used his infamy as a narcotics-addled whoremonger who was fired from his TV sitcom, *Two and a Half Men*, to bilk the public in one of the wilier chump-change scams in recent memory. Sheen's loon-ball "Charlie Sheen Live!: My Violent Torpedo of Truth/Defeat Is Not an Option" tour blew into Denver on this date, following its debut in Detroit on April 2 and stops in Chicago, Atlanta, Atlantic City, Cleveland, Dallas and other cities. *The Hollywood Reporter* noted that, at the Detroit show, "Sheen was booed off stage by a hostile crowd after delivering a poorly planned show filled with faux-Biblical preaching and extended video clips." The act had Charlie and his rants and a couple of underdressed bimbos, whom he dubbed his "goddesses," performing lesbian kissing exhibitions. Sheen talked about his marriages and legal problems. About his preference for paying prostitutes for sex, the forty-five-year-old son of Martin Sheen said, "I have millions to blow, and I ran out of stuff to buy." What a life.

APRIL 29

1935—GOODNESS HAD NOTHING TO DO WITH IT

Mae West's only film in the year of her reign as the "highest paid woman in the United States" and "second highest paid person in the U.S." behind publisher William Randolph Hearst was *Goin' to Town*, released this week. It followed the Depression-era successes of *Night After Night* (1932), *She Done Him Wrong* (1933), *I'm No Angel* (1933) and *Belle of the Nineties* (1934), all of which kept Paramount Pictures afloat in the Depression. The National Legion of Decency and the Production Code were chasing their definitions of immorality off the screen just as West's saucy, suggestive shtick gained popularity. She had risen to fame on Broadway as the writer, star and director of *Sex* (1926). Critically panned, the play seduced the public until the cast, crew and company were charged with obscenity in February 1927. West spent ten days confined to Welfare Island and was fined $500, ensuring her national notoriety.

APRIL 30

1970—FARMER'S DAUGHTER BUYS THE FARM

The beautiful, blonde, Swedish-born star of ABC-TV's family sitcom *The Farmer's Daughter* from 1963 to 1966, Inger Stevens died in an ambulance on its way to the hospital on this date. The Los Angeles County coroner called the cause of death "acute barbiturate poisoning." Stevens had been distraught over her secret marriage to African American actor-executive Ike Jones, an employee from the 1950s through the 1970s for companies owned by Burt Lancaster, Harry Belafonte and Nat King Cole. The Jones-Stevens union was secretly performed in Tijuana, Mexico, at a time when black-white marriages were considered incendiary and career suicide. She was attempting resumption of home-tube stardom after a series of window-dressing film roles—*Firecreek* (1967) with James Stewart, *Hang 'Em High* (1968) with Clint Eastwood, *House of Cards* (1969) with George Peppard—when the end arrived. She was thirty-six.

MAY 1

1941—HEARST WHO GETS SLAPPED

RKO Radio Pictures released writer-director-producer-star Orson Welles's *Citizen Kane* in New York City on this date. The film's parallels to the life of newspaper magnate William Randolph Hearst were obvious. One of America's most influential tycoons and a master of yellow journalism, Hearst was furious at the unflattering portrayal of himself and ordered his newspapers to ignore the film but eventually acquiesced. "With one brain cell working, the Chief realized that such hysterical barking by the trained seals would attract too much attention to the picture," wrote Robert Shaw, a former Hearst Newspapers critic. The twenty-four-year-old "boy genius" Welles and his co-screenwriter, Herman J. Mankiewicz, vividly portrayed a Hearstian-style newspaper empire and the publisher's romance with a much younger entertainer in the manner of Hearst and mistress Marion Davies. The nature of the film was a hot topic all spring, but the impartial cognoscenti judged it a masterpiece upon release—and ever since.

MAY 2

1997—EDDIE'S TRANSVESTITE HOOKER

As wisecracking tough guys go, Eddie Murphy was flush with currency as an action star after the *Beverly Hills Cop* and *48HRS* franchises. *The Nutty Professor* (1996) was out, and Eddie reigned as the greatest success story of the *Saturday Night Live!* performers in movies. Then he was stopped by the Los Angeles County Sheriff's Department just before 5:00 a.m. on this date, driving his wife's SUV on Santa Monica Boulevard in West Hollywood. The deputies followed Murphy after he picked up a transvestite hooker named Atisone Kenneth Seiuli (aka Shalomar). They stopped Murphy, gabbed, got his autograph and let him go but arrested Seiuli on an outstanding warrant for violating probation on a prostitution charge. The incident made the papers, and Eddie claimed to be a good Samaritan in the wee hours, giving Seiuli a lift. The following week, Tim Meadows starred in an *SNL* skit as Eddie, ferrying a carload of transvestite hookers around Hollywood. Almost a year later, on April 22, Seiuli died in a fall after he tried to enter the fifth-floor window of his locked LA apartment. He was twenty-one.

MAY 3

1947—THE MOTHER WAS…DIVORCED!

The National Legion of Decency condemned three films in 1947: the saucy *Forever Amber*; the portrayal of missionary nuns, *Black Narcissus*; and that vile bag of garbage *Miracle on 34th Street*. This enduring yuletide classic from an original story by Valentine Davies concerned a Macy's-employed Kris Kringle at Christmastime going on trial to prove to a disbelieving little girl (Natalie Wood) that he, indeed, was Santa Claus. Released on this weekend, the film eventually earned Oscars for best supporting actor for Edmund Gwenn's Santa and for the writing of Davies and director George Seaton. However, the legion's priests complained that the film offered a sympathetic treatment of the girl's divorced mother, played by Maureen O'Hara. In the strictest sense of Catholic mores, divorce equaled failure and disgrace. When O'Hara was heaved and humiliated for ten minutes by John Wayne across Irish landscapes in John Ford's *The Quiet Man* (1952), to the delight of a wagering priest, it was okay by the legion.

MAY 4

2001—NAME O' DIS TUNE IS MOIDAH

Robert Blake used to be best known as the perching shoulder for a big cockatoo named Fred in the 1970s ABC-TV police drama *Baretta*. On this date, he escorted his second wife, Bonny Lee Bakley, to her final dinner at Vitello's Restaurant in Studio City and found himself on the other end of the law. While seated alone in Blake's car after dinner, Bakley was killed by a gunshot to the head. After walking her to the car, Blake claimed he returned to the pasta joint for a gun that he had left there and was not present at the killing. This gun proved to not fire the fatal shots. Blake was charged in the murder a year after the fact but was acquitted. Bakley's children then filed a civil suit against Blake, saying he was responsible for the death. In 2005, a jury found Blake liable for the wrongful death, and an appeals court upheld the verdict but slashed the original $30 million payment in half. Blake, who quit acting, went bankrupt. As for Bonny Lee, her ten marriages ended in five annulments, four divorces and her death. She was forty-four.

MAY 5

1968—FETISH-FEST EXIT, STACKED BY DEKKER

Albert Dekker served in the California State Assembly for the 57th Assembly District from 1944 to 1946 and later famously spoke out against the smear tactics of Senator Joseph McCarthy during the latter's infamous Communist witch hunts. Dekker was the title character in *Dr. Cyclops* (1940), battled John Wayne in *In Old Oklahoma* (1943) and acted with James Dean in *East of Eden* (1955). Dekker's last film was released posthumously; he played the mean-browed leader of the ragtag posse who pursued *The Wild Bunch* (1969). On this day, about a decade after his sixteen-year-old son, Jan, accidentally shot himself to death in Hastings-on-Hudson, New York, Dekker was found in his bathroom naked, kneeling, hanged, bound, blindfolded, gagged and handcuffed, with obscene lipstick messages on his body. The Los Angeles County coroner ruled Dekker's end as accidental, and the cause was "autoerotic asphyxiation." Dekker was sixty-two.

MAY 6

1994—BOBCAT LIGHTS UP LENO

Would you put in charge of *anything* a screaming guy named Bobcat who purposefully sets things on fire? Well, Robert Francis Goldthwait, aka "Bobcat," a formerly screeching and guttural stand-up comic from Syracuse, New York, has costarred in dozens of movies and *directed* hundreds of shows and films, including 250-plus episodes of *Jimmy Kimmel Live!*, 42 episodes of *The Man Show* and what publicity materials shamelessly called "the *Citizen Kane* of alcoholic-clown movies"—*Shakes the Clown* (1991). Bobcat used to set things on fire, more literally than figuratively. On this date, Bobcat was a guest at a taping of *The Tonight Show with Jay Leno*. He lit the guest chair on fire and then extinguished the flames. He was fined $2,700 plus the $700 cost of the chair. Bobcat also was required to tape public service announcements concerning safety and pay the City of Burbank $500 for all the fuss. The stunt was the basis of the plot for Bobcat's subsequent appearance on *The Larry Sanders Show*.

MAY 7

Kiefer Sutherland, who kept TV's espionage wars alive from 2001 to 2010 as the intrepid Jack Bauer on *24*, surrendered to New York City cops on this date for head-butting fashion designer Jack McCollough, who had interrupted the actor's conversation with Brooke Shields at the Mercer Hotel bar. Weeks later, Sutherland and McCollough issued a joint statement in which Sutherland apologized. Police dropped the assault charges. A similar script was followed at the Mercer, this SoHo hotbed of celeb fuming, when Russell Crowe became peeved in the wee hours of June 6, 2005, because he couldn't seem to make a call to Australia and caromed a telephone off the concierge's face. The Oscar winner for *Gladiator* (2000) and the star of the Oscar-winning best picture *A Beautiful Mind* (2001), Crowe settled out of court with the concierge for a six-figure sum. The Manhattan district attorney dropped the assault charges.

MAY 8

1955—HAPPY MOTHER'S DAY! FROM FRANK

The actual Mother's Day of 1955 occurred on this date, and the following true story came out years after the fact in magazine articles. While making *Not as a Stranger*, Robert Mitchum and Frank Sinatra shared the marquee and their dressing rooms with a third rover, Broderick Crawford, who turned all three preparatory chambers into a bar. One morning just prior to Mother's Day weekend, Big Bad Bob arrived early to find Frank on the hospital set on his back on an operating table, still in his dinner jacket. Bob, a very accommodating sort when it came to beverages, mixed up a bloody Mary and connected it to the saloon singer's lips via a pliant hospital sipper, and the liquid level descended. Frank, sufficiently nourished and still prone, intoned, "Mother!" For more than four decades, or until Mitchum died in 1997, Frank sent him annual Mother's Day cards.

MAY 9

1991—BOMBSHELL IN COKE BUST

Italian actress Laura Antonelli was never one to let clothing remain in the way of acting. The former athletics instructor wore her birthday suit in many sexually charged romantic melodramas in the 1970s and 1980s: *The Divine Nymph* (1975), *Wifemistress* (1977), etc. Her incursions into the American market were on the cheap-jack side, with Vincent Price in *Dr. Goldfoot and the Girl Bombs* (1966) and in director Vic Morrow's *A Man Called Sledge* (1970) with James Garner. Antonelli was arrested on this date and confined to house arrest on charges of cocaine possession and trafficking. She was convicted and sentenced to three years and six months in prison. Antonelli spent ten years appealing the conviction, which was eventually overturned.

MAY 10

1968—*OUR GANG* TO THE WRONG GANG

Scotty Beckett was an *Our Gang* series regular as "Scotty," goofing around with Spanky, Alfalfa and Buckwheat. As a child and teen actor, he was very busy, playing the title role as a youth in *The Jolson Story* (1946) and acting post-teen roles in *Battleground* (1949), *The Happy Years* (1950) and many other movies, as well as the radio series *The Life of Riley* and the TV series *Rocky Jones, Space Ranger* (1954). But Scotty's increasingly erratic behavior led to a DUI in 1948, elopement with tennis star Beverly Baker in 1949 and charges of check fraud and carrying a concealed weapon. Two marriages and divorces later, Scotty entered a Hollywood nursing home, requiring medical attention for wounds he received from a vicious beating. He never left. Pills and a note were found, but no conclusion was made by the LA County coroner as to the exact cause of death. Speculation was a combo of alcohol and barbiturates. Scotty was thirty-eight.

MAY 11

1999—HOISTING A FEW FOR OLIVER REED

The burly British star of *Oliver!* (1968), *Women in Love* (1970) and *Castaway* (1987) expired of a heart attack on Malta, appropriately in a bar, on May 2, 1999. Oliver, a lifelong pub crawler extraordinaire, had downed three bottles of Captain Morgan's Jamaica rum, eight bottles of German beer, doubles of Famous Grouse whiskey and Hennessy cognac and had bested five much younger Royal Navy sailors at arm wrestling. His bar bill was 270 Maltese lira, or about $705. He was on location, costarring in the Russell Crowe–fronted *Gladiator* (2000). Between his fatal heart attack and burial service in his native County Cork, Ireland, near Churchtown, his grave site was prepared on this date in Bruhenny Cemetery, in full view of his favorite pub. An especially unapologetic imbiber, Reed, the death jape went, required little embalming. On May 15, more than one thousand mourners sang "Consider Yourself One of Us" from *Oliver!* at the funeral, after which the "mother of all parties" was thrown. Oliver was sixty-one.

MAY 12

1958—MONTY'S TRAUMATIC CRASH

One of the most admired actors of his generation, and a contemporary of Marlon Brando and James Dean, Montgomery Clift was nominated for Oscars for *The Search* (1948), *A Place in the Sun* (1951) and *From Here to Eternity* (1953). A closeted gay man and frequent boozer and drug abuser, Monty was leaving a dinner party at best pal Liz Taylor's Beverly Hills home on this date when he plowed his car into a utility pole. Liz heard the crash and came running. She pulled two of his teeth out of his throat so he could breathe, saving his life. Filming ceased for six weeks on *Raintree County* (1957), which starred Clift and Taylor, while Monty's

face was reconstructed and he convalesced. His pre-crash and post-crash scenes are discernible in the finished film. He never really recovered. Clift picked up a last Oscar nomination as a concentration camp survivor in *Judgment at Nuremburg* (1961), but the increased booze and narcotics after the accident, plus other lingering maladies, did him in. He died in New York of a heart attack at forty-five.

MAY 13

1933—Wifey Dearest Divorces

Joan Crawford's first hubby was Douglas Fairbanks Jr., the son of Hollywood royalty Douglas Fairbanks and stepson of "America's Sweetheart," Mary Pickford. Generations before Joan became known for coat hanger–wielding abuse via her daughter Christina's 1978 book exposé, *Mommie Dearest*, the former Lucille Fay LeSueur from San Antonio, Texas, clawed her way to stardom in *Our Dancing Daughters* (1928). None other than F. Scott Fitzgerald proclaimed her the epitome of the Jazz Age flapper, but that didn't make her welcome at Pickfair. The Fairbanks-Crawford union in 1929 New York City was opposed by Doug Sr. and Mary, who waited eight months to invite the newlyweds to their Pickfair manse. Crawford divorced Fairbanks on this date, citing "grievous mental cruelty," as well as "a jealous and suspicious attitude." Doug Jr. married twice more; Joan hitched three more times, twice to actors Franchot Tone and Phillip Terry and then to Pepsi-Cola CEO Alfred Steele.

MAY 14

2000—To His Own Self, He's True

John Travolta believed in the philosophy of Scientology and trusted his convictions. One of those was that the script for *Battlefield Earth: A Saga of the Year 3000* would make a fabulous sci-fi tribute to Scientology guru L. Ron Hubbard, who wrote the source novel. A former Catholic, Travolta had converted to Scientology, as had Tom Cruise, Nicole Kidman and Mimi Rogers. *Battlefield Earth*, released on this weekend, didn't proselytize for Scientology but certainly stank from moldy melodrama. Costing $95 million to make and sell, including producer Travolta's own millions, *Battlefield Earth* grossed $21 million in domestic revenue. Critic Elvis Mitchell, looking toward ninety-nine years of cinema ahead, wrote in the *New York Times*, "*Battlefield Earth* may well turn out to be the worst movie of this century." Travolta's stardom survived through such hits such as *Swordfish* (2001), *Wild Hogs* (2007), *Hairspray* (2007)…

MAY 15

1999—DRUG-ADDLED DICK CRACKS UP

At about 10:45 a.m. on this date, actor and comedian Andy Dick lost control of his automobile and careened into a utility pole while allegedly driving under the influence. The costar of *Bongwater* (1997), *Dude, Where's My Car* (2000) and other films, Dick tried to run away from the scene on Highland Avenue in Los Angeles's Hancock Park neighborhood. He was detained for police by a witness. The cops found marijuana and cocaine in Dick's car, arrested the actor on DUI and drug possession charges and released him on $10,000 bail. He later pleaded no contest to the charges and entered rehab. Dick has since been arrested at least eight times in four states, usually for being drunk or for lewd behavior. He was escorted off a Canadian stage for exposing himself and thrown out of a pornographic-films awards show. He appeared in 2009 on *Sober House* and *Celebrity Rehab with Dr. Drew*.

MAY 16

2011—THE "GOVERNATOR'S" LOVE CHILD

The *Los Angeles Times* reported on this date that former California governor, movie star and bodybuilding champion Arnold Schwarzenegger had fathered a son out of wedlock more than fourteen years earlier with a household employee, Mildred Patricia "Patty" Baena. "After leaving the governor's office I told my wife about this event, which occurred over a decade ago," Schwarzenegger said in a statement. He didn't mention that he had confessed to his wife, former TV host and Kennedy clan peripheral Maria Shriver, only after she had confronted him with the information. Baena, a former Guatemalan national, was employed by the family for twenty years and retired in January 2012. The pregnant Baena was working in the home while Shriver was pregnant with the youngest of the couple's four children. Baena's son with Schwarzenegger, Joseph, was born on October 2, 1997. Shriver and Schwarzenegger separated after twenty-five years together on May 9, 2011.

MAY 17

1987—*ISHTAR* MEANS DISASTROUS

In Asian cultures, the term "Ishtar" references a goddess of love and fertility. After this weekend in 1987, it signified, as Hollywood scribe James Robert Parish pointed out, "colossal, embarrassing Hollywood film flop with…no redeeming aspects." Made by Columbia Pictures for $51 million, *Ishtar* earned back $14 million in domestic rentals. Starring Warren Beatty and Dustin Hoffman in desert shenanigans written and directed by Elaine May, *Ishtar* was designed as a Hope/Crosby-style "road" movie, but it lacked charm or humor. The stars were too old for camel jokes, and the dialogue was embarrassing. Critic Roger Ebert wrote that *Ishtar* was a "lifeless, massive, lumbering exercise in failed comedy." Beatty survived to do *Dick Tracy* (1990) and *Bugsy* (1991) and add Madonna and Annette Bening to his conquests; Hoffman to win an Oscar for *Rain Man* (1988); and May to garner a nomination for writing *Primary Colors* (1998).

MAY 18

1984—MOON? MORE LIKE MARS

Andy Kaufman was one of the more unfathomable Hollywood cult legends. None of the cast of his show, *Taxi* (1978–1983), attended his funeral on this date in Great Neck, New York. He had died of lung cancer on May 16 at Cedars-Sinai Medical Center. His one starring film role was as a robot in *Heartbeeps* (1981). He often showed up in full-body disguise as his alter ego, Tony Clifton, a boozy insult comedian, even on *The Tonight Show Starring Johnny Carson*. Andy's writing partner, Bob Zmuda, has said he also played Tony Clifton in various appearances where assumptions were that Tony was Andy. Andy was an Elvis Presley impersonator, performed a one-man show at Carnegie Hall and wrestled professionally. Milos Forman directed Jim Carrey in *Man on the Moon* (1999), about Andy's life. Some mourners at the open-casket service saw just another Kaufman ruse and poked the body. He was thirty-five.

MAY 19

1961—Just a Little Back Pain

Jeff Chandler was a distinctive action star of the 1950s who three times enacted Apache legend Cochise, including to an Oscar nomination in *Broken Arrow* (1950). During production on director Sam Fuller's *Merrill's Marauders* (1962), Chandler hurt his back in a baseball game with U.S. infantrymen, who were extras in the film. After the picture, Chandler entered Culver City Hospital on May 13 for an operation for a spinal disc herniation. He never left. The operation ruptured an artery, and a nearly eight-hour second operation followed, and then another operation after that. He went through eighty pints of blood through it all, about seven times the amount in the normal male body. He was listed in critical condition on this date and by June 17 was dead. Tony Curtis and Gerald Mohr were among the pallbearers. The malpractice settlement benefited Chandler's children. The hospital, branded "the Jeff Chandler hospital," changed its name. Chandler was forty-two.

MAY 20

1998—ONE DAY IN THE LIFE OF CHARLIE SHEEN

Charlie Sheen overdosed on cocaine by injecting it on this date and was admitted to Los Robles Regional Medical Center in Thousand Oaks, California. Paramedics were called at 4:20 a.m. to an emergency at Sheen's Malibu home and indicated that the thirty-three-year-old actor had suffered a possible stroke. Sheen had been complaining of a tingling sensation and loss of feeling in his extremities. Charlie was placed in the intensive care unit. Martin Sheen stopped by to check on the prodigal and assured the Charlie-watch press that the star of *Platoon* (1986), *Wall Street* (1987) and many other big-screen productions "is very much alive" and "doing very well." Marty urged Charlie fans to show support "in this very difficult time." Charlie soon traipsed to another quick shuffle in his lifelong rehab tango and made more movies and TV shows.

MAY 21

1943—Ava and Mickey Call It Quits

Not long after nineteen-year-old Ava Lavinia Gardner of Grabtown, North Carolina, arrived in Los Angeles to become a Metro-Goldwyn-Mayer contract player, she married diminutive MGM star Mickey Rooney on January 10, 1942, in Ballard, California. They divorced on this date. He was the twenty-one-year-old star of the Andy Hardy series, a mom-and-apple-pie vision of small-town America; she was window dressing for several years until her breakout performance in *The Killers* (1946). Rooney claimed the couple had a rip-roaring sex life. Gardner said that she didn't particularly think of it in the same terms and once characterized their marriage as "Love Finds Andy Hardy"—the title of a 1938 Rooney/MGM hit. Ava liked them sawed-off, later marrying bandleader Artie Shaw and Frank Sinatra. Rooney remarried seven more times.

MAY 22

1981—CASUALTY OF *WORLD WAR III*

The only known film or television director to have been killed on location in the performance of his profession, Boris Sagal left the living on this day at Timberline Lodge, Oregon, on the slopes of Mount Hood. He was directing scenes in *World War III* (1982), an NBC-TV movie starring Rock Hudson. The Ukrainian-born Sagal accidentally walked into the spinning tail rotor blade of a helicopter, which nearly completely decapitated him, killing him instantly. Sagal had received Emmy Award nominations for directing the miniseries *Rich Man, Poor Man* (1976) and *Masada* (1981), and his theatrical pictures included *Girl Happy* (1965) with Elvis Presley and *The Omega Man* (1971) with Charlton Heston. Among Sagal's survivors were his wife, former MGM dancer Marge Champion, and their daughter, Katey Sagal, who followed them into the business and is best known as Peg Bundy on *Married With Children*. Boris Sagal was fifty-seven.

MAY 23

2005—CRUISE CONTROL GONE

Megastar Tom Cruise began dating actress Katie Holmes in April 2005. The star of TV's *Dawson's Creek*, Holmes seemed a rather well-scrubbed match for the toothsome Tom Terrific. The christened Thomas Cruise Mapother IV of Syracuse, New York, was a guest on *The Oprah Winfrey Show* on this date and, dressed completely in black, declared his love for Katie in a rather outlandish manner, hugging Oprah, squeezing her hands, kneeling before her, pounding the floor, jumping up on her couch, throwing his arms to the sky, clutching the victory fist and shouting, "I'm in love!" The crowd screamed. The official and unofficial psychiatrists wandering close to their TV sets at home paused. Noted Scientology follower Cruise's display, known as the "Couch Incident," was voted the No. 1 "Most Surprising TV Moment" of 2005 on E! Entertainment Television.

MAY 24

1950—INGRID'S ROMAN HOLIDAY

Ingrid Bergman was the epitome of Hollywood beauty and talent in *Casablanca* (1943), *Gaslight* (1945), *Notorious* (1946) and other classics—and then her affair with Italian director Roberto Rossellini flamed in Italy during production on *Stromboli* (1950). While both were married, she to Swedish physician Petter Lindstrom, the coverage of the affair evolved into a watershed mark in tabloid journalism. Photographs of Roberto and Ingrid holding hands appeared in the worldwide press. Ingrid denied to syndicated columnist Hedda Hopper that she was pregnant with Rossellini's child, but rival scribbler Louella Parsons announced the pregnancy days later. Hopper, incensed, repeatedly slammed Ingrid in print. Ed Sullivan refused to allow the actress on his TV show. Ingrid was denounced on the floor of the U.S. Senate by Edwin C. Johnson of Colorado as a "free-love cultist" and an "instrument of evil." Ingrid survived it all to win two more Oscars, for *Anastasia* (1956) and *Murder on the Orient Express* (1974).

Ingrid Bergman starred in *For Whom the Bell Tolls* (1943) with Akim Tamiroff (left) and Gary Cooper.

MAY 25

1995—MADAM TO THE STARS

A sting operation coordinated among the Los Angeles and Beverly Hills Police Departments and the U.S. Justice Department netted the reigning madam to the stars, Heidi Fleiss. Her supposed little black book of names, phone numbers and sexual proclivities of the rich and famous was suspected for causing hives among a portion of the Hollywood galaxy. She sent three hookers with cocaine in June 1993 to satisfy a clientele of four, who were actually undercover agents. The twenty-seven-year-old Fleiss was arrested and charged with pandering, pimping and narcotics possession. She pled not guilty and protected her clientele at the trial, even though Charlie Sheen testified. She was found guilty on three pandering charges by a California court and then convicted on eight of fourteen counts of conspiracy, money laundering and tax evasion in federal court. Heidi was sentenced by Los Angeles Superior Court judge Judith Champagne on this date to three years in prison. She eventually spent thirty-seven months in federal prison (see January 7).

MAY 26

Actress Lindsay Lohan was arrested on this date after swerving her 2005 Mercedes Benz into a curb. She entered rehab. On July 24, Lohan was arrested for speeding after another vehicle in Santa Monica and charged with drunk driving, driving with a suspended license and cocaine possession. On August 23, the star of such movies as *Freaky Friday* (2003), *Confessions of a Teenage Drama Queen* (2004) and *Mean Girls* (2004) pleaded guilty to cocaine use and driving under the influence and was sentenced to a day in jail, community service, fines, an alcohol education program and three years' probation. At a July 6, 2010 hearing, a judge determined that Lohan had violated her probation and was sentenced to ninety days in jail. She served thirteen days and was ordered into rehab. After failing a drug test on September 17, 2010, Lohan spent fifteen hours in jail and was freed on $300,000 bail. She checked into rehab for the fifth time on September 28, 2010.

MAY 27

2011—RAVAGES OF DRUG ABUSE

Jeff Conaway's movies include *Grease* (1978) and dozens of low-budget items, such as *Bikini Summer II* (1992), which he also directed. His recurring TV roles include those on *Taxi* and *Babylon 5*. But drug and alcohol abuse, particularly cocaine and painkillers, rendered him sometimes unable to work. He was a rehab-tango regular and appeared on *Celebrity Rehab with Dr. Drew*. Found unconscious on May 11, 2011, Conaway was rushed to Encino-Tarzana Regional Medical Center, where he was listed in critical condition. The diagnoses were pneumonia accompanied by sepsis, the inflammation of his whole body. He was induced into a coma to fight the infection. He was taken off life support on May 26 and died on this date. He had aspirated, and germs from his mouth infected his lungs. Encephalopathy was an accompanying cause, since his liver quit and couldn't fight the toxins in his blood stream. He was sixty.

MAY 28

1998—PHIL HARTMAN: GUNNED IN BED

The "*SNL* Curse" dogs veterans of NBC's *Saturday Night Live!*, which began airing in 1975. This curse, in which the grim reaper takes comics years before their time, has claimed John Belushi, Gilda Radner, Andy Kaufman, Danitra Vance, writer/producer Michael O'Donoghue, Chris Farley, Charles Rocket and, on this date, Phil Hartman. Hartman was fatally shot to death in his sleep at his Encino, California, home by his wife, Brynn, who later committed suicide. Specializing in impressions of President Bill Clinton on *SNL*, Hartman also created striking versions of Ronald Reagan, Charlton Heston and Frank Sinatra. Hartman was known as the "glue" who kept the *SNL* cast and crew together, according to former cast member Adam Sandler. Hartman also played the egotistical radio newsman Bill McNeal on the sitcom *NewsRadio*. He was forty-nine.

MAY 29

1995—Madonna's Stalking "Husbands"

A stalker climbed over the wall of Madonna's former estate, Castillo del Lago, off Mulholland Drive on this date and was shot three times in a struggle with an armed guard employed by the singer-actress. The first possibility to rule out in any Madonna stalking is that the perpetrator was forced to watch her inane pictures: *Shanghai Surprise* (1986), *Who's That Girl* (1987) and *Body of Evidence* (1993). However, the guy claimed to have been the performer's husband. The stalker was convicted and sentenced to a prison term. This was the second time that a stalker on the property had claimed to be Madonna's hubby and the second time one had been sentenced to jail. The yellow-and-black striped terra cotta home in the Hollywood Hills, located below the Hollywood(land) sign, once was a gambling casino run by LA racketeer Bugsy Siegel.

MAY 30

1969—X-Rated Film Wins Best Picture Oscar

Director John Schlesinger's *Midnight Cowboy*, starring Dustin Hoffman and Jon Voight as Times Square bums, premiered in New York during this week. It went on to win the Academy Award for best picture and became the only X-rated film to win any Oscar, let alone best picture. (Only one other X-rated film was ever nominated in any category, Stanley Kubrick's *A Clockwork Orange*, 1971.) The film's craftsmanship and merits were up for discussion for the rest of 1969 as bluenoses wondered whether the Academy of Motion Picture Arts & Sciences would honor a film that the Motion Picture Association of America had deemed akin to pornography. Their worst fears were confirmed when the film was conferred with seven nominations and then three Oscars early in 1970: the film, Schlesinger and screenwriter Waldo Salt won. After the X flap, the MPAA broadened the requirements for the R rating to allow more content and raised the age restriction from sixteen to seventeen. *Midnight Cowboy* was then rated R for its 1971 reissue with no edits made.

Jon Voight (left) and Dustin Hoffman costarred as unlikely friends in John Schlesinger's *Midnight Cowboy* (1969).

MAY 31

1994—HOPPER GETS RIPPED, TWICE

Gabbing on *The Tonight Show with Jay Leno* on this date, Dennis Hopper told a story of the old days when he directed Peter Fonda, Jack Nicholson and himself in the classic *Easy Rider* (1969). Hopper claimed that Rip Torn was originally cast as the boozy lawyer in the film, the part that eventually brought Jack his first Oscar nomination. Hopper claimed on the show that Rip pulled a knife on him during pre-production, leading to the Ripster's ouster from the project. In 1997, Torn filed a defamation lawsuit against Hopper over the story. Rip's suit claimed that Hopper was the one who pulled the knife on him. Hopper was ordered to pay $475,000 in punitive damages after a judge ruled in Torn's favor. Hopper's appeal brought a double-whammy: another judge again ruled in Torn's favor, requiring Hopper in 1999 to pay another $475,000 in damages.

JUNE 1

1971—*TO HELL AND BACK*, THEN VIRGINIA

The bodies of Audie Murphy and five companions were found on this date on Brush Mountain, near Roanoke, Virginia, following the crash of a private plane. The nation mourned the loss of the most decorated soldier of World War II. His twenty-four honors included the Medal of Honor for a 1945 battle at Holtzwihr, France, in which he was wounded and crawled atop a burning tank destroyer to fire a .50-caliber machine gun, routing hundreds of German soldiers. He starred in westerns and the adaptations of *The Red Badge of Courage* (1950) and his own war exploits, *To Hell and Back* (1954). Murphy was acquitted in 1970 of attempted murder, and creative speculation connected the plane crash

to his campaign to get Teamsters racketeer Jimmy Hoffa released from prison. Director Don Siegel sought Murphy to play "Scorpio" in *Dirty Harry* (1971), reasoning he might as well hire the greatest killer of them all. Murphy's death sent the role to Andy Robinson. Murphy was buried with full military honors on June 7 in Arlington National Cemetery. He was forty-six.

JUNE 2

2001—"The Reviewer Who Wasn't There"
Newsweek reporter John Horn tracked the rave movie reviews of one David Manning of the *Ridgeview Press*, which highly touted such generally mediocre films as *Hollow Man*, *Vertical Limit* and *A Knight's Tale*. Horn's story, published on this date, concluded that Sony Pictures had not stopped at making up critical raves but made up the critic and his newspaper, further skewing into outright fraud the studio blurb-meister mill, in which raves are coerced from not-so-reluctant reviewers who like to see their names on movie posters. The studio publicity department apologized for the hoax. Four years after the fact, a lawsuit led to a court order on August 3, 2005, for the studio to refund five dollars to anyone disappointed by the pictures that "Manning" hailed and who had attended them because he or she was duped into doing so by the raves signed by the hoax name.

JUNE 3

2008—An Old Flame Burns Again

For the eighth time, the Universal Pictures back lot caught on fire. The previous seven fires in 1932, 1949, 1957, 1967, 1987, 1990 and 1997 had burned different portions of the giant moviemaking lot and theme-park attraction, located in its own municipal footprint near Burbank. Arson was suspected in some of the fires, but the big one in 2008 was the result of a welding accident. The three-alarm fire took more than five hundred firefighters aided by water-dropping helicopters twelve hours to subdue. Low water pressure was blamed for the delay in putting out the blaze on June 1. Nothing irreplaceable was lost, according to studio executives on this date, and the sets and theme-park exhibits that were damaged were replaced with $50 million in new buildings and features, including the *King Kong* exhibit based on the 2005 Peter Jackson film.

JUNE 4

Other celebs were worse actors, kookier drunks and more desperate for jobs than Bowen Charlton Tufts III. It's just that these traits coalesced around "Sonny" Tufts, who died of pneumonia in Santa Monica on this date. Descended from the Boston blueblood banking family that founded Tufts University, Sonny married Spanish dancer Barbara Dare and costarred in *So Proudly We Hail* (1943), *Easy Come, Easy Go* (1947), *The Seven Year Itch* (1955) and others. He was arrested for walking the yellow line in a Hollywood Street. Two exotic dancers sued him for chomping their thighs. When he lost the role of Jim Bowie in *The Alamo* (1960) to the director, John Wayne, it devastated him. Pop-

culture references to Sonny included those on *The Dick Van Dyke Show*, *My Mother the Car* and *The Monkees*, and he appeared as himself on *Rowan & Martin's Laugh-In*. When Boris Badenov swipes Bullwinkle's autographed picture of Sonny Tufts on *Rocky and His Friends*, the moose becomes very upset. Sonny Tufts was fifty-eight.

JUNE 5

1957—WHALE OF A DIRECTOR

The great horror film director James Whale was found
floating in his swimming pool on May 29, 1957. A suicide
note described his nerves as being shot. The narcotics he
was taking after two strokes and bouts with depression
seemed in the previous months to have hastened the decline
of his mental faculties. One of the cinema's true geniuses,
Whale had retired from the film business after a round-
robin of contretemps with Nazi emissaries and Universal
Pictures over the content of his World War I epic, *The
Road Back* (1937), the sequel to *All Quiet on the Western Front*
(1930). Whale's imaginative conception and execution of
otherworldly terrors in *Frankenstein* (1931), *The Old Dark
House* (1932), *The Invisible Man* (1933), *Bride of Frankenstein*
(1935) and other films concerning the animation of the
dead found no entry to his own corpse at Gates, Kingsley
& Gates Mortuary on this date. He was cremated the
following day. The final days of the gay Whale's life were
portrayed by Ian McKellen in director Bill Condon's *Gods
and Monsters* (1998). Whale was sixty-three.

JUNE 6

1937—BLONDE BOMBSHELL'S FINAL DAYS

Jean Harlow's illnesses had delayed production on *Wife vs. Secretary* (1936), *Suzy* (1936) and *Libeled Lady* (1936). The press kept tabs on such things while she filmed *Saratoga* (1937) with Clark Gable. Conflicting reports on the actress, who made her reputation playing brassy floozies in such pre–Production Code pictures as *Platinum Blonde* (1931), *Red Dust* (1932) and *Bombshell* (1933), said she either had the flu or that a more debilitating malady was taking her down. She turned down a dinner date with former costar William Powell on this night and was rushed to Good Samaritan Hospital in Los Angeles, where she slipped into a coma. She died the following day, June 7, of cerebral edema complicated by kidney failure. *Saratoga* became MGM's biggest hit of 1937, owing to Harlow's legion of fans. Her life was portrayed in two so-so 1965 films, both called *Harlow*, one with Carroll Baker and the other starring Carol Lynley. Jean was twenty-six.

JUNE 7

1993—WOODMAN LOSES CUSTODY

Hanky-panky with the adopted daughter of a longtime lover might be judged morally reprehensible in most quarters. To writer-director Woody Allen's life and film collaborator, Mia Farrow, it was a gargantuan obscenity. She found out in January 1992 about the affair between Allen and her South Korean–born adoptive daughter, Soon-Yi Previn, who had joined her brood during her marriage to composer André Previn. Mia's famous artistic collaboration with Allen, which produced such well-regarded films as *Purple Rose of Cairo* (1985), *Hannah and Her Sisters* (1986), *Husbands and Wives* (1992) and others, was torn asunder and qualified as premium tabloid fodder for three reasons: the Woodman's fall from grace, Mia's reactionary anger and the thirty-four-year difference in the secret lovers' ages. During the nasty custody battles for their three children, which Allen lost on this date, Mia accused Woody of child molestation, which was never proven. Allen and Soon-Yi married on Christmas Eve 1997 in Venice, Italy.

JUNE 8

1999—SECOND AMENDMENT GODFATHER

Charlton Heston brought *The Ten Commandments* (1956) down off the mountain, flogged a chariot race into film immortality as *Ben-Hur* (1959), found earth's future to be *Planet of the Apes* (1968) and helped turn the tide of World War II in *Midway* (1975). Elected president of the National Rifle Association on this date in Philadelphia, Chuck evinced political convictions that have always been actively complex—marching in person in Dr. Martin Luther King Jr.'s civil rights campaigns, picketing a theater showing his

own *El Cid* (1961), turning down an offer to run for the U.S. Senate and switching from Democrat to Republican. At the 2000 NRA convention, Chuck raised a rifle over his head and said that a then potential Al Gore administration would take away his Second Amendment rights "from my cold, dead hands." George W. Bush defeated Gore for the presidency, saving Chuck from a chilly and early earthly exit. Chuck didn't go to that biblical epic in the sky until it apparently was time, on April 5, 2008. He was eighty-four.

JUNE 9

1980—THE HUMAN TORCH

A mind-bending combination of cocaine and rum pushed one of America's edgiest funnymen over the edge on this date in the Los Angeles suburb of Northridge. Richard Pryor was filming *Bustin' Loose* (1981) when his cranial screws reflected that title. After free-basing cocaine while knocking back a little 151-proof rum, Richard poured the rum on his body and set himself on fire. His daughter, Rain Pryor, later called the episode a case of drug-induced psychosis. Pryor ran out of the house and down Parthenia Street like a flame-thrower victim in a war picture. In the inverse of the cliché that says there's never a cop around when you need one, patrolling police spotted the scurrying flame ball and put Pryor out. He was hospitalized and treated for burns covering most of his body. After six weeks in recovery at the Grossman Burn Center in Sherman Oaks, California, Pryor incorporated a description of the incident into his comedy *Richard Pryor: Live on Sunset Strip* (1982), the operative term being "live."

JUNE 10

1985—"Brat Pack" Unleashed

The term comes from the headline over David Blum's cover story in *New York Magazine* on this date. It was loosely applied to a group of young actors who were hot at the time because of their clubby appearance as day-to-day pals in the movies *The Breakfast Club* and *St. Elmo's Fire*. To many of the core actors, it has been a pejorative term, something to ignore and outgrow. These players include Emilio Estevez, Anthony Michael Hall, Rob Lowe, Andrew McCarthy, Demi Moore, Judd Nelson, Molly Ringwald and Ally Sheedy. The article swung wide to nick Matthew Broderick, John Cusack, Robert Downey Jr. and Tom Cruise. Obviously, the term is derivative of the Rat Pack, Frank Sinatra's moveable bender of nightclub swingers from the 1960s. Most of the Brat Packers have sustained rewarding careers. Snags set back Lowe and Downey, but nothing approaching the tabloid spectacle of Emilio's younger bro, Charlie Sheen.

JUNE 11

1934—INDECENCY FASCINATES PRIESTS

A parochial decision to censure the nation's film industry gathered national momentum on this date when *Time* magazine colluded with the National Legion of Decency to severely undermine Hollywood filmmakers and studio bosses, and thus millions of Americans on a weekly basis. "For many a year the U.S. churches have deplored what they call the brazen indecency of U.S. cinema," *Time* chided. "Last week, led by members of the Roman Catholic Church, they were embarked on a new crusade, brandishing a new weapon—the boycott." Priests were to decide the films the people would see by condemning and boycotting those they disliked. Founded in 1933 by Archbishop of Cincinnati John T. McNicholas, this repressive group felt dirty pictures corrupted youth and urged the purification of Hollywood product. The Motion Picture Producers and Distributors of America headed off complete outside meddling by policing its own ranks, establishing the finalized Production Code (see June 13 and July 1).

JUNE 12

1994—O.J.'s Wife and Friend Slain
Los Angeles homicide lore includes some dillies: William Desmond Taylor, the Black Dahlia, Bugsy Siegel, Johnny Stompanato, the Tate-LaBianca Murders, the Menendez brothers, Robert Blake's wife, etc. But no single murder generated international media interest the way the one that occurred on this date did. Actor and former athlete O.J. Simpson's ex-wife, Nicole Brown Simpson, and her lover, Ronald Goldman, a waiter and aspiring actor, were found stabbed to death in LA's Brentwood neighborhood. O.J., "the Juice," was the gifted African American athlete who made good, from USC Heisman Trophy–winning halfback to NFL Hall of Famer to TV and movie star, notably as Detective Nordberg to Leslie Nielsen's Frank Drebin in the hijinks of *The Naked Gun* franchise. Even with some strong evidence, the LA County DA's prosecutorial team couldn't quite convince the jury that O.J. did it. See October 3.

JUNE 13

1934—HOLLYWOOD POLICES ITS RANKS

In the first reaction to the establishment of the National Legion of Decency (see June 11), an amendment to a preexisting Production Code was adopted by the Motion Picture Producers and Distributors of America on this date. Responding to criticisms over racy studio films, the MPPDA established the Production Code Administration and required pictures to obtain a certificate of approval before release (see also July 1). Joseph I. Breen was named head of the administration, and he enforced the new cleansing of the celluloid: no illicit drugs, homosexuality, premarital sex, profanity, prostitution, white slavery or interracial relationships or marriage. Breen had the power to change scripts, which drove many in Hollywood's creative community toward increased creative suggestion of naughtiness to the audience. Among the first order of business was cutting nude scenes of Maureen O'Sullivan, playing Jane, from *Tarzan and His Mate* (1934).

JUNE 14

1989—Zsa Zsa to the Clink

Occasional actress and full-time socialite Zsa Zsa Gabor, whose nine husbands included hotelier Conrad Hilton and actor George Sanders, slapped a Beverly Hills police officer on this date at the corner of Olympic Boulevard and Le Doux Road. He had pulled her over to write a ticket. She claimed he used rude language, for which she cracked him one across the chops. He arrested her for assault on a police officer, disobeying a police officer, driving without registration, driving without a license and having a flask of bourbon in the glove compartment. Miss Hungary of 1936, the star of John Huston's *Moulin Rouge* (1952) and the sister of *Green Acres* star Eva Gabor, Zsa Zsa was sentenced to three days in jail on the assault conviction. The incident was parodied in at least three movies, including *The Naked Gun 2½: The Smell of Fear* (1991).

JUNE 15

1977—SIR DICKIE'S "MILLION DOLLAR HOUR"

The World War II epic *A Bridge Too Far* entered theaters on this date, and its publicity illuminated the cost of large-scale moviemaking to the public as it portrayed a giant Allied operation behind German lines in 1944. Director Sir Richard Attenborough's handling of the logistics on the morning of October 3, 1976, on the actual war setting, Nijmegen Bridge over the River Waal, was described by screenwriter William Goldman, who quoted an assistant director's order: "Corpses, listen now, you corpses, all corpses will keep eyes shut at all times while the cameras are rolling, you got that?—not one bloody blink from one bloody corpse and that's final!" No second take was scheduled: $1 million of the $27 million picture was allotted for 8:00 to 9:00 a.m. that day, when Dutch authorities granted use of the bridge and stopped river traffic, and Robert Redford, the priciest actor in the cast, earned his money. Bridge, Redford, cast, crew, stunts, explosives, boats, tanks, trucks, ceased traffic—all cost more than $1 million.

JUNE 16

1959—Faster Than a Speeding Bullet!

But not this time. George Reeves, who had rocketed to fame as the title character in TV's *The Adventures of Superman* from 1952 to 1957, was found shot in the head with a nine-millimeter Luger on this date in his Benedict Canyon home. The death was ruled a suicide. Before his fame as the comic-book superhero, the former Golden Gloves boxer had managed to score small parts in big films, including *Gone with the Wind* (1939) and *From Here to Eternity* (1953). But he became so identified with the tights and cape that after the series was over, he couldn't find other parts to play. His distress at this situation has often been blamed for his despair. His family rejected the coroner's ruling and believed Reeves was murdered. Reeves was laid to rest in the same business suit that he wore as Clark Kent.

JUNE 17

1963—Denial Along the Nile

The most expensive movie ever made up to this date premiered this week in New York City. Director Joseph L. Mankiewicz's gargantuan *Cleopatra* starred Liz Taylor in perhaps the ultimate example of a movie out of control, managed by the fix-it process of heaving more money at production problems. The picture lumbered across the screen with a cast of thousands and a cost of $42 million, or something around $260 million in twenty-first-century dollars. The picture made back $26 million at the domestic box office and sent Twentieth Century-Fox floundering in debt through the 1960s. At 243 minutes, it dragged on for a posterior-cramping eon, 5 minutes longer than *Gone with the Wind* (1939). On the set, Liz and Dick Burton dallied, divorced their significant others and began their tabloid saga. Although it won four Oscars, *Cleopatra* was Hollywood's last giant money drain...until *Paint Your Wagon* (1969)... or *Heaven's Gate* (1980)...or *Last Action Hero* (1993)...or *Cutthroat Island* (1995)...or *John Carter* (2012)...

JUNE 18

1969—IMPACT OF *THE WILD BUNCH*

Director Sam Peckinpah's epic western about aging outlaws pulling their final job and pursued by an American posse into an uneasy alliance with Mexican *federales* south of the Rio Grande became the second major American studio production after Arthur Penn's *Bonnie and Clyde* (1967) to push the envelope as far as violence in films. The director punctuated the bloody shooting deaths by using slow motion in the manner of NFL Films. The final shootout is a masterwork of filmmaking with set design, cinematography, editing, acting and direction coalescing into a masterly whole. But the reception by critics and the public was as mixed as it could be—appreciation and condemnation side by side. Certain viewers couldn't abide the bloodletting. William Holden and the entire cast are superb in this bona fide masterpiece. If the film weren't so engaging and pictorially stunning, and the characters so vivid and the entire story so compelling, no one would have cared. Today, the violence seems quaint.

JUNE 19

1962—NABOKOV'S, KUBRICK'S *LOLITA*

Director Stanley Kubrick's film of Vladimir Nabokov's novel concerns a divorced professor who marries a love-starved woman because he has fallen in lust with her pre-teen daughter. The picture, in its first week of release in New York on this date, stirred less controversy after the fact than it did before its release. The Motion Picture Association of America, which approved scripts in those days, insisted that the age of Lolita be raised from twelve to early teens, and Kubrick agreed. Sue Lyon was hired for the role over Tuesday Weld, as well as Hayley Mills and Joey Heatherton, who turned it down through their fathers, and Jill Haworth was denied the opportunity by her contract holder, Otto Preminger. Lyon possessed a more mature look (she was fourteen at the time) than the others. Cognizant of what the National Legion of Decency did to submarine a somewhat similar older-man/teen-girl theme in *Baby Doll* (1956), Kubrick relied on suggestion more than erotic contact. Still, the picture created a mild fuss.

JUNE 20

1947—Bugsy Siegel Gunned Down

Benjamin Siegel lived with the mob and died by its methods. Los Angeles's highest-profile mobster of the 1930s and 1940s, Bugsy was racketeer to the stars, invited to lavish parties, consorting with Jean Harlow, Ketti Gallian and Virginia Hill. But he didn't make money fast enough for the mob in the new racket of Las Vegas, so he was killed in the Beverly Hills mansion of B-movie starlet Hill on this date. Siegel was shot through a window by a still unknown assailant. Bugsy had been very active in the postwar mob vision of Vegas as a cash cow. Siegel invested in *Hollywood Reporter* founder and owner Billy Wilkerson's Flamingo Hotel and then stole it for syndicate control under the threat of death to the publisher, who went into hiding in Europe. Trouble was, Bugsy couldn't generate cash fast enough, so he got the business end of an M1 carbine, events re-created by director-producer-star Warren Beatty in *Bugsy* (1990).

JUNE 21

1982—JOHN HINCKLEY JR.: NOT GUILTY

The son of a Dallas oil tycoon who shot President Ronald Reagan and three others with a .22-caliber revolver on March 30, 1981, outside the Hilton Hotel in San Francisco, was found not guilty of thirteen crimes by reason of insanity on this date. The verdict posed the question: which was the bigger scandal, Hinckley's world-shaking violent act or the verdict? Hinckley said his motive was to impress actress Jodie Foster and called his assassination attempt "the greatest love offering in the history of the world." Hinckley had been obsessed with the actress since she portrayed a twelve-year-old hooker in Martin Scorsese's *Taxi Driver* (1976), in which the protagonist contemplates the assassination of a politician. Since the verdict, Hinckley has been incarcerated at St. Elizabeth's Hospital in Washington, D.C., and in recent years has been allowed to visit his parents in Williamsburg, Virginia. Former actor Reagan died in 2004 from pneumonia. Jodie, who rebuffed Hinckley's approaches when she attended Yale University, went on to win Oscars for her performances in *The Accused* (1988) and *The Silence of the Lambs* (1991).

JUNE 22

1969—WE'RE NOT IN KANSAS ANYMORE

Judy Garland was found dead on this date by her fifth husband, Mickey Deans, in the bathroom of their rented house in the Chelsea section of London. Coroner Gavin Thursdon said the cause of death was an "incautious self-over-dosage" of barbiturates. Judy's blood contained the equivalent of ten 1.5-grain (97 milligram) Seconal capsules. Thursdon stressed that no evidence pointed to suicide. The autopsy showed that the drug had been ingested over time, rather than in one dose. It was an accidental OD. She was forty-seven. Ray Bolger, her costar in *The Wizard of Oz* (1939), said, "She just plain wore out." On June 26, Deans took Garland's remains to New York City, where an estimated twenty thousand people lined up for hours at the Frank E. Campbell Funeral Home to pay their respects. On June 27, James Mason, Judy's costar in *A Star Is Born* (1954), delivered the eulogy at the funeral. She was interred in a crypt in Hartsdale, New York.

JUNE 23

1998—FRANK WOULD HAVE CLOBBERED THE PUNKS

Frank Sinatra's last LA abode was on Foothill Road in Beverly Hills. On this night—five weeks after Frank finally flew to the moon (on May 14, 1998), after gradual heart ailments and what was termed in Hoboken and everywhere else a particularly nice life—his widow, Barbara, and her son, Robert Marx, walked back home after dinner. Accompanying them were the retired former producer of *Rowan & Martin's Laugh-In*, George Schlatter, and his wife. On the Doheny Road sidewalk, the group was mugged by three punks demanding valuables. The victims complied but were attacked by one of the men, who launched into a karate pose and kicked at Schlatter. The sixty-five-year-old producer grabbed the attacker's leg and flipped him over. A fight broke out. Marx was struck, the women's purses were nabbed and the robbers fled. One of the items stolen included a gift of jewelry from Frank to Barbara.

JUNE 24

Despite having given up cigarettes for a decade, actor Brian Keith suffered from emphysema and lung cancer in his final years, and the pain, plus the suicide of his daughter, Daisy, two months before this date, was believed to have moved him to end it all. He was found dead on this date of a self-inflicted gunshot wound in his home on Malibu Colony Road in Malibu. Keith was best known to television audiences as Uncle Bill on CBS-TV's *Family Affair* from 1966 to 1971 and also starred in the series *The Brian Keith Show*, *Hardcastle & McCormick* and *Heartland*, as well as several hit films, including *The Parent Trap* (1961), *The Russians Are Coming, the Russians Are Coming* (1966) and *The Wind and the Lion* (1975), in which he portrayed Teddy Roosevelt. The Bayonne, New Jersey native, who had married three times, was seventy-five.

JUNE 25

1965—THE LAST VOYAGE OF STEVE COCHRAN

Cochran was a noticeable presence in big movies—*The Best Years of Our Lives* (1946) and *White Heat* (1949)—and a rough presence in rough pictures such as *Storm Warning* (1951) and *Private Hell 36* (1954). This date marked his tenth day in his roughest-ever state—decomposition—surrounded by hysterical women aboard his schooner, *The Rogue*. Guatemalan authorities discovered the drifting craft and guided it into the Pacific port of Champerico. Steve, whose affairs included those with Mae West, Joan Crawford, Merle Oberon, Mamie Van Doren, Ida Lupino and Kay Kendall, had expired on June 15 after keeping *The Rogue* afloat for two days and nights during a hurricane. He had advertised

for an all-women crew in *Variety* to make a movie aboard the yacht, but the first group abandoned ship at Ensenada, Mexico, so he had hired the Mexican replacements for $5.83 a day at Acapulco. The cause of death was acute infectious edema. Some speculated the body wasn't Cochran's, but nobody's seen him since. He was forty-eight.

JUNE 26

1974—Liz and Dick Call It Quits

The number-one couple on the gossip and social radars for a generation, frequent costars Elizabeth Taylor and Richard Burton divorced on this date. It marked her fourth split after those from hotel heir Nicky Hilton, actor Michael Wilding and pop singer Eddie Fisher (another one, producer Mike

Todd, died in a plane crash). It was Dick's second divorce after his split with Sybil Williams. The Liz and Dick marital spat was often likened to their remarkable onscreen drinking bout in Mike Nichols's film of Edward Albee's *Who's Afraid of Virginia Woolf?* (1966), for which she won her second Oscar. They costarred ten times, including in *Cleopatra* (1963), *The V.I.P.s* (1963), *The Sandpiper* (1965) and *The Taming of the Shrew* (1967). Their pairing in the TV movie *Divorce His—Divorce Hers* (1973) proved very prophetic indeed.

Richard Burton (front) starred with Peter O'Toole in *Becket* (1964).

JUNE 27

1995—Hugh Grant Arrested

Hugh Grant was out looking for some action on Sunset Boulevard and found more than he bargained for on this date when his solicitation for escort services from Hollywood prostitute Divine Brown led to the exchange of $60 for oral sex in his car. A policeman noticed the brake lights flash on the car several times and investigated. He arrested the actor for lewd conduct, and Grant pleaded no contest and was sentenced to attend an AIDS class and perform five days of community service. Brown, whose real name was Estella M. Thompson, was fined $1,150 and sentenced to four months in jail for parole violations. Grant said he had no excuses for his bad behavior, including on *The Tonight Show with Jay Leno*, and never was defensive about the incident. His successful films after the incident included *Sense and Sensibility* (1995), *Notting Hill* (1999), *Bridget Jones's Diary* (2001) and others.

JUNE 28

1955—STANLEY'S "10 WEEKS OF HELL"

Producer Stanley Kramer's first picture as a director, *Not as a Stranger* (1955), was released in New York on this date. Robert Mitchum, who starred as an unscrupulous physician, said, "It wasn't so much a cast as a brewery." Broderick Crawford, who had won an Oscar for *All the King's Men* (1949), converted the male stars' dressing rooms into a bar by ripping off the connecting doors, which suited Mitchum and Frank Sinatra and found no protests from thirsty cast members Gloria Grahame, Lee Marvin, Myron McCormick and Lon Chaney Jr. One escapade was unique in potable annals: "Brod Crawford…drank Sinatra's [hair] piece," Mitchum recalled. "We were trying to pull it away from him. He got this hairpiece halfway down, and he takes a glass of vodka and downs the goddamn thing. So, I called Frank—Frank was in Palm Springs—I said, 'Guess what? The Crawdad just drank your wig.' He said, 'Good, I don't have to show up on Monday.'" Kramer called the shoot "10 weeks of hell."

JUNE 29

1978—BOB CRANE'S BEATEN BODY

The bludgeoned body of actor Bob Crane—the star of ABC-TV's *Hogan's Heroes* from 1965 to 1971 and its spinoff movie, *The Wicked Dreams of Paul Schultz* (1968), as well as the Disney pictures *Superdad* (1973) and *Gus* (1976)—was found in a Scottsdale, Arizona hotel room on this date. Superdad was a sex addict whose relationships and involvement in pornography were portrayed in Paul Schrader's film *Auto Focus* (2002), starring Greg Kinnear. Crane had been playing in a dinner theater production. The murder remains unsolved, but police suspected Crane friend and video technician John Henry Carpenter during the initial investigation, when no murder weapon was recovered and only circumstantial evidence was available. Crane and Carpenter conspired in the surreptitious filming of their sexual conquests. When the case was reopened by the Maricopa County district attorney in 1994, Carpenter was tried for the murder and acquitted. He was portrayed in the Schrader film by actor Willem Dafoe as sexually attracted to Crane. Carpenter died in 1998.

JUNE 30

1970—*MYRA BRECKINRIDGE* RELEASED

A candidate for the worst film of all time, *Myra Breckinridge* was based on Gore Vidal's namesake novel about a transsexual. Raquel Welch starred with John Huston, Mae West and Farrah Fawcett. The perpetrator of this morass of sex jokes was writer-director Michael Sarne, a British pop singer and actor. "This is a horrifying movie, but not because it's dirty," wrote Joe Morgenstern in *Newsweek*. "It's horrifying because it's an entirely incompetent, impotent attempt at exploitation by an industry that knew once, at the very least, how to make a dishonest buck." *Time* magazine infamously called the film "about as funny as a child molester." The film, which died at the box office after a week in release on this date, earned an X rating from the Motion Picture Association of America.

JULY 1

1934—THE PRODUCTION CODE

The movies were decidedly too violent and sexy for tastemakers of the early 1930s. James Cagney, Edward G. Robinson and Paul Muni rose to fame playing racketeers. The suggestive sexual escapades of Mae West, Marlene Dietrich and Barbara Stanwyck were barely suggestive anymore. The Motion Picture Producers and Distributors of America finally put its collective foot down, neutering the entire industry on this date before someone else did it for it. The MPPDA enacted the Production Code, which governed the content of studio pictures for decades thereafter. Prodded by the forming of the Catholic-based National Legion of Decency earlier the same year, the code was enforced so that "no picture shall be produced which will lower the standards of those who see it." Sympathy for crime and sinning was discouraged, and forbidden were "excessively lustful kissing," seduction, rape, miscegenation, venereal disease, sex organs, cursing, etc. The promiscuity of such pre-code films as *Red Dust* (1932), *Baby Face* (1933) and *The Story of Temple Drake* (1933) became a thing of the past.

JULY 2

1996—ANOTHER HEMINGWAY SUICIDE

On the thirty-fifth anniversary of the death of Ernest Hemingway, the master novelist's granddaughter, model and actress Margaux Hemingway, was found dead inside her Santa Monica apartment. Once called the "Face of a Generation," the six-foot star of *Lipstick* (1976) and other films and the face of the Faberge fragrance Babe had been dead for days and her body decomposed. Margaux had been through a divorce from filmmaker Bernard Foucher, sifted through fewer and fewer magazine cover offers and mediocre movie roles, posed for *Playboy* and been in and out of the Betty Ford dry-out tank. The eldest daughter of Ernie's son, Jack Hemingway, one-time Idaho Fish and Game commissioner, she became the fifth member of her family to take his or her own life. The cause of death was an overdose of sedatives. She was forty-one. Her ashes are buried in the shadow of her grandfather's monument in Ketchum, Idaho.

JULY 3

1967—BLONDE BOMBSHELL LAID TO REST

Jayne Mansfield's burial took place on this date in Bryn Mawr, Pennsylvania, where she was born thirty-four years earlier as Vera Jayne Palmer. The voluptuous actress and former *Playboy* model was killed instantly on June 29, 1967, when the speeding Buick Electra in which she was riding with her lawyer, Sam Brody, and her three children struck the rear of an insecticide truck spraying the roadside on U.S. 90 near the Rigolets Bridge in southeastern Louisiana. Mansfield, who had starred in *The Wayward Bus* (1957) and *Will Success Spoil Rock Hunter?* (1957), was on her way in the wee hours from an appearance at the Gus Stevens Dinner Club in Biloxi, Mississippi, to one on an early-morning New Orleans television show. Indications were that the Buick, driven by Ronald Harrison, might have been going eighty miles per hour. The three adults were killed. The three kids, asleep in the backseat, were injured but survived. The youngest, three-year-old "Marie," aka Mariska Hargitay, grew up to become the star of *Law & Order: Special Victims Unit*.

JULY 4

1968—THE DUKE AND VIETNAM

The Green Berets, John Wayne's slightly right of right-wing war picture about an unpopular American conflict, released at the height of that southeast Asia debacle, received its world premiere on the Fourth of July in Atlanta, not far from where much of it was filmed at Fort Benning, Georgia. The picture was pilloried by critics for its application of the jingoistic rhetoric of other times, the World War II and early cold war eras, to an Asian civil war that eventually cost fifty-eight thousand American lives. A joke to the campus crowd, which vigorously protested the war across America, the film was still a popular hit. The Duke co-directed the picture as well as starred, and he took heat for it the rest of his life. It didn't dent his box-office appeal, mostly in westerns, and he won the Oscar for best actor the following year for *True Grit* (1969).

JULY 5

1948—SEXY REXY: A LADY-KILLER

The body of actress Carole Landis was found on this date on the bathroom floor of her Pacific Palisades home, an apparent suicide from an overdose of sleeping pills. She had spent the night with Rex Harrison, who refused to break up his marriage to actress Lilli Palmer to become the twenty-nine-year-old Landis's fourth husband. A shapely beauty born Frances Lillian Mary Ridste in Fairchild, Wisconsin, on New Year's Day 1919, Landis had been a teen nightclub hula dancer and singer in San Francisco and had starred in *One Million B.C.* (1940). Carole's family always suspected that the suave Rex had something to do with her demise. He had burned the photos of their relationship and instructed his lawyers to destroy her suicide note to him. Far from representing the literal interpretation of his later title role as *Doctor Dolittle* (1966), Sexy Rexy was diddle-do and ran through six wives, including actresses Kay Kendall and Rachel Roberts.

Rex Harrison starred with Audrey Hepburn in *My Fair Lady* (1964).

JULY 6

1960—Battleaxe Bette Dumps Last Hubby

Bette Davis told a Portland, Maine judge on this date of her husband Gary Merrill's decade of "cruel and abusive treatment" and was granted a divorce. Merrill failed to appear at the hearing, and indications were that he failed to appear in the marriage. Bette later quipped, "Gary was a macho man, but none of my husbands was ever man enough to  become Mr. Bette Davis." Merrill, who costarred with her in *All About Eve* (1950), was the last hubby with whom she bothered. Davis, who won Oscars for *Dangerous* (1935) and *Jezebel* (1938), counted *Dark Victory* (1939), *The Letter* (1940) and *The Star* (1952) among her ten Oscar nominations. "Until you're known in my profession as a monster," she said, "you're not a star." When she started at Universal, an executive quipped that she had "as much sex appeal as Slim Summerville." After rising through Warner Bros., she became known for the "perfect figure." Things change in Hollywood. Bette acted through *The Whales of August* (1987). She died of breast cancer on October 6, 1989.

JULY 7

1946—FLYBOY HOWARD HUGHES DROPS IN

Like his film producing career and crowded romantic history, Howard Hughes's pioneering aviation exploits contained some bumps, none more harrowing than his impromptu crash-landing on this date at 808 North Linden Drive in Beverly Hills. Engine trouble developed in the experimental XF-11, and Hughes, flying solo, tried to set the crate down on Los Angeles Country Club fairways. But the airplane skipped off a couple of roofs and careened into the house at 808, burning it to the ground. The crash crushed Howie's collarbone, cracked ribs, punctured a lung and shifted his heart to the right side of his chest cavity, and he suffered third-degree burns. The tycoon's recovery hooked him on opiates, and his eccentric life grew a little more erratic. Director Martin Scorsese immortalized the moment with star Leonardo DiCaprio in *The Aviator* (2004).

JULY 8

1965—LAST FLIGHT OF PAUL MANTZ

In one of Hollywood's more notable stunt tragedies, renowned production pilot Paul Mantz was killed on this date among the dunes of Buttercup Valley, about twenty miles from Yuma, Arizona. He was flying for a camera retake on director Robert Aldrich's *The Flight of the Phoenix* (1965) starring James Stewart. Mantz's vast experience included stunts for John Ford's *Air Mail* (1932) and Henry King's *Twelve O'Clock High* (1949). Mantz was flying the crate built to replicate the one in the film, which, in novelist Elleston Trevor's and the film's plot, was devised by a toy engineer and built by the survivors of a downed cargo plane in the Sahara Desert. One of the skids on the cobbled-together plane caught the ground and it toppled, killing Mantz and throwing co-pilot Bobby Rose to the ground. Rose survived. Mantz was sixty-one.

JULY 9

One of the watershed moments of American exploitation filmmaking crystallized as *Shaft* entered its second week of wide release. Richard Roundtree starred as John Shaft, an African American private eye who's hired to find the kidnapped daughter of a Harlem racketeer. As the bodies dropped or were exposed, the "blaxploitation" genre was launched if not yet so identified, confirming what Melvin Van Peebles's independently made *Sweet Sweetback's Baadasssss Song* (released in April 1971) was implying with record-breaking box-office takes in Detroit and Atlanta: the black, urban market was a lucrative one to court directly. The sequels arrived: *Shaft's Big Score* (1972) and *Shaft in Africa* (1973, advertised as "The Brother-man in the Motherland"). A virtual flood tide of dark urban adventures followed: *Blacula* (1972), *Superfly* (1972), *Black Gunn* (1972), *Cleopatra Jones* (1973), *Black Caesar* (1973), *Black Eye* (1974), *Foxy Brown* (1974), etc. New stars were created in Pam Grier, Fred Williamson, Ron O'Neal and others.

JULY 10

1973—"PEEK-A-BOO" SEX SYMBOL'S LUSH LIFE

Veronica Lake's "peek-a-boo" wavy locks over one eye were replicated by cartoonists for Jessica Rabbit in *Who Framed Roger Rabbit* (1988) and by Kim Basinger in her Oscar-winning performance in *L.A. Confidential* (1997). Lake, née Constance Frances Marie Ockelman, from Brooklyn, starred in *Sullivan's Travels* (1941), *This Gun for Hire* (1942) and *The Blue Dahlia* (1946). Arrested twice in the 1950s for public drunkenness, by 1962, Veronica was a bartender at the all-girls' Martha Washington Hotel in Manhattan. Sporadic TV work interrupted the imbibing. She died on July 7, 1973, of renal failure caused by hepatitis in a Burlington, Vermont hospital. Her body was cremated on this date at the Mount Pleasant Cemetery in St. Johnsbury, Vermont, and the ashes sat on a shelf for three years due to nonpayment. They were either scattered in the waters off Dade County, Florida, in 1976, according to her wishes, or, as an urban legend persists, remain in the possession of a New York writer. Lake was fifty.

JULY 11

1997—SPIELBERG'S LOONY STALKER

A bodybuilder with two previous felony arrests and an obsession with Steven Spielberg was arrested on this date outside the filmmaker's Pacific Palisades mansion. The visitor toted a bag containing handcuffs, duct tape and a box cutter, as well as *Jurassic Park* memorabilia and a shopping list of sadomasochistic items, including "three dog collars." The stalker's auto contained a scrapbook with photos of Spielberg and his family, a list of the director's associates and razor blades. This scary interloper was thirty-one-year-old Jonathan Norman, who had been conspicuous around the premises on prior occasions and wanted to show Spielberg—the director of some of the biggest Hollywood films of all time, including *Jaws* (1975) and *E.T.: The Extra-Terrestrial* (1982)—a lurid script he had written about "a man raping another man." Through the trial and conviction on stalking charges, it was revealed that Norman's goal was to tie up Spielberg's wife, actress Kate Capshaw, and make her watch while he raped her husband. Norman was convicted in less than four hours and sentenced to twenty-five years to life in March 1998.

JULY 12

1973—ALI AND STEVE MAKE IT OFFICIAL

About a month after Ali MacGraw divorced Bob Evans, who put her most famous picture, *Love Story* (1970), into production as head of Paramount Pictures, she married her costar in *The Getaway* (1972). She and Steve McQueen were hitched on this date in a city park in Cheyenne, Wyoming, while on location for director Sam Peckinpah's *The Getaway*. Steve bolted his marriage to former dancer Neile Adams. The Steve-Ali union lasted five years, during which Ali wanted to return to the biz, but Steve, a macho dude, philanderer and heavy drinker, said absolutely not. She divorced him and hitched a ride on Peckinpah's *Convoy* (1978). Steve died of a heart attack after cancer surgery just two years later. Meanwhile, Bob survived seven marriages and more controlled substances than we'll ever know. Ali remains single.

JULY 13

The infamous Otto Preminger film *The Moon Is Blue* went into its first full week of wide release on this date after its premiere in New York. The picture was the first studio-produced film to deliberately bypass approval from the Production Code. It also became the first studio film condemned by the National Legion of Decency to turn a profit. The corrupting salaciousness that would corrode American ideals concerned William Holden and David Niven as womanizers with one goal—the deflowering of Maggie McNamara, a lass in the Audrey Hepburn mold. The film's dialogue boldly used the verboten terms "virgin" and "pregnant." She vowed to remain a virgin until her wedding night. McNamara received an Oscar nomination, Niven won the Golden Globe and the picture proved to Hollywood that the code could be broken.

JULY 14

1972—HANOI JANE: GOOD MORNING, VIETNAM!

Jane Fonda won an Oscar for *Klute* (1971) and would win another, for *Coming Home* (1978), before and after her stint as a spokesperson for antiwar protesters of the Vietnam era. On this date, broadcasting live from Hanoi, where she was a guest of the North Vietnamese Communist government, she inspired a depth of hatred that has never abated in many of the U.S. troops who heard her broadcast. "This is Jane Fonda speaking from Hanoi, and I'm speaking particularly to the U.S. servicemen," she said. "I don't know what your officers tell you…but [your] weapons are illegal and that's not just rhetoric…The men who are ordering you to use these weapons are war criminals according to international law, and in the past, in Germany and Japan, men who committed these kinds of crimes were tried and executed." Henry Fonda's daughter later cashed in with exercise videos and married TV mogul Ted Turner. However, for many a dogface, jarhead, airman and swabby, Fonda will forever be known as the traitorous "Hanoi Jane."

JULY 15

1935—MARY ASTOR'S DIRTY DIARY

A superb performer who won the Oscar for best supporting actress in *The Great Lie* (1941), Mary Astor achieved lasting notoriety for her brilliant turn as the deceiving dame to Humphrey Bogart's private eye in *The Maltese Falcon* (1941). Astor was at the center of perhaps the biggest Hollywood scandal of the 1930s after she countersued her husband, Dr. Franklyn Thorpe, on this date to retain custody of their four-year-old daughter, Marylyn. Thorpe's attorneys threatened to enter her diary into the proceedings, which detailed her extramarital liaisons with other celebrities, especially her trysts with playwright George S. Kaufman.

While the diary was sealed by the court, its existence and possible contents became newspaper fodder for weeks, causing a case of Hollywood-wide nervousness. The diary was later destroyed with Astor's permission. Her next film, *Dodsworth* (1936), was a substantial hit, and she worked steadily for three more decades.

Mary Astor is left center in *The Palm Beach Story* (1942) with Joel McCrea (left) and Claudette Colbert and Rudy Vallee.

JULY 16

1997—Bob Downey Jr.: Less Than Zero

Lisa Curtis returned to her home on Heathercliff Road in Malibu on this date and found a strange man passed out in one of the beds. The police were called, and the stranger was identified as her neighbor, actor Robert Downey Jr., star of *Air America* (1990), *Chaplin* (1992) and many other films. The arrest was only the most infamous Downey incarceration through the succeeding, very hazy years. The son of director Robert Downey told one judge that his dad gave him the stuff and that he had used narcotics since age eight. Violating parole and sentencing became repetitive. In August 1999, Downey was slapped with three years in prison but was released in 2000 for cumulative time served. Arrests followed; police found him wandering barefoot in Culver City in 2001. Uncharacteristically for such an addict, Downey regained his career in spectacular fashion, including in *Iron Man* (2008), *Sherlock Holmes* (2009) and *The Avengers* (2012).

JULY 17

1999—OLIVER STONE DOUBLE-STONED

Anti-establishment filmmaker Oliver Stone was released on $12,500 bail on this date after Los Angeles police arrested him on Benedict Canyon Drive before midnight the previous day for drunk driving and felony possession of hashish. The cops had followed him from Wilshire Boulevard. Stone was pulled over for moving violations while driving his Ford Mustang. The writer-director's pictures include the Turkish hash-bust thriller *Midnight Express* (1978); the booze-guzzling war correspondent saga *Salvador* (1986); and the dope-smoking Vietnam War dramas *Platoon* (1986) and *Born on the Fourth of July* (1989). Few have ever blamed Oliver's gritty films for not being authentic. Oliver pleaded no contest to the DUI and possession charges and received a suspended sentence in return for entering rehab.

JULY 18

1994—MICKEY RUMBLES WITH THE WIFE

Mickey Rourke, who has often been seen in a "wife-beater," imitated his undergarment on this date by slapping, knocking down and kicking Carré Otis, his wife and costar in *Wild Orchid* (1989). The former prizefighter was arrested by the LAPD on a charge of misdemeanor spousal battery. The star of *Diner* (1981), *Angel Heart* (1987), *Barfly* (1987) and other pictures was ordered to stand trial, but Otis skipped the court dates and the charges were dropped. Carré had previously been shot in the shoulder in New Mexico by a gun registered to Rourke; she claimed it went off accidentally. The two separated and divorced in 1998. Rourke, also a former nightclub bouncer, was arrested in 1994 in Miami for a disturbance in which he cursed and aggressively threatened a crowd outside his own nightclub. He was arrested on a DUI charge on November 8, 2007, while riding a motor scooter. Rourke received an Oscar nomination for his "comeback" role as Randy "The Ram" Robinson in *The Wrestler* (2008).

JULY 19

Francis Albert Sinatra, fifty, married Mia Farrow, twenty-one, on this date after he proposed to the star of TV's *Peyton Place* on Loveladies Beach at Long Beach Island, New Jersey. The two had met on the set of Frank's World War II epic, *Von Ryan's Express* (1965), and the marriage was his third of four. The tabloid press emphasized the older man/younger woman angle: Frank, doing it his way, again. Mia hadn't yet zoned into her earth-mother phase, for which she was well known during her later marriage to musician André Previn and her relationship with Woody Allen. She had promised to costar with Frank in *The Detective* (1968) but signed instead for director Roman Polanski's creepy horror film *Rosemary's Baby* (1968). After she refused to quit Polanski's picture and do *The Detective*, Frank served her with divorce papers on the horror film's set. Lee Remick costarred in *The Detective*.

JULY 20

1973—BRUCE LEE EXPIRES

He was the most influential martial artist of the twentieth century and the man most responsible for changing the way in which the reserved and stoic cliché of the Asian male was perceived by Hollywood. But Bruce Lee suddenly went to his maker on this date. One of the most stunt-friendly and obviously outwardly physically fit of all actors, in such films as *Fist of Fury* (1972) and *Enter the Dragon* (1973), Lee expired at the Hong Kong home of actress Betty Ting. He had taken the painkiller Equagesic, which contained muscle relaxants and aspirin. When producer Raymond Chow, visiting Ting, could not wake Lee, an ambulance was called. The actor died on the way to Queen Elizabeth Hospital. "Death by misadventure" was the official ruling, but Lee suffered an acute cerebral edema due to a reaction to compounds in Equagesic. Lee's pallbearers on July 31 included Steve McQueen, James Coburn, Chuck Norris and George Lazenby.

JULY 21

1978—GROUP-JEOPARDY SUBGENRE STUNG

Airport (1970) resurrected the mothball plot of a boatload of stars in jeopardy, and producer Irwin Allen seized on the boatload idea with *The Poseidon Adventure* (1972). Then came *Earthquake* (1974), *The Towering Inferno* (1974), *Juggernaut* (1974), *Airport 75* (1975), etc. The worst of these suspense epics with pre-fab plots is certainly Allen's *The Swarm* (1978), which sank in its second week of release on this date. Allen directed (for the second time in his career) a plot about Africanized killer bees poised to attack Houston while military and environmentally sound solutions are weighed. Bee stings are preferable to the dialogue. "Houston on fire…" contemplates Richard Widmark's general. "Will history blame me or the bees?" Blame Irwin. He lost so much money that he forbade his employees to ever mention the film.

JULY 22

1965—AN AFFAIR TO REMEMBER

Cary Grant and Dyan Cannon eloped to Las Vegas on this date and got hitched in the Dunes Hotel. Debonair Cary was sixty-one, the starlet twenty-seven. He noticed her on television in the series *Malibu Run*. The quickie wedding was followed by a first-half honeymoon to Bristol, England, where Grant informed his mother of his fourth wife. The previous three were actresses Virginia Cherrill and Betsy Drake and troubled socialite Barbara Hutton. The fifth, in 1968, was public relations agent Barbara Harris. The Grant/Cannon second-half honeymoon was spent at 10050 Cielo Drive, Beverly Hills, where the Manson clan murdered Sharon Tate and four others four years later. Cary and Dyan had a daughter, Jennifer. Dyan left the union in 1966, citing his bad temper and contending that he spanked her. Cary retired, and her career heated up with *Bob & Carol & Ted & Alice* (1969), *Heaven Can Wait* (1978) and *Deathtrap* (1982).

JULY 23

1982—VIC MORROW AND TWO CHILDREN

In one of the most shocking accidents in Hollywood history, actor Vic Morrow and two children were killed during an after-midnight shoot at Indian Dunes Park near Santa Clarita, California. The children, Myca Dinh Le and Renee Shin-Yi Chen, portrayed Vietnamese, and Morrow enacted a bigot during a Vietnam War scene in the John Landis–directed *Time Out* segment of producer Steven Spielberg's *Twilight Zone—The Movie* (1982). Morrow carried the kids while wading into a river as fireballs were detonated. A helicopter twenty-four feet above the actors spun out of control when two explosions went off. Renee, who had slipped from Morrow's grasp, was crushed by the copter as it dropped into the river. Vic and Myca were decapitated by the rotor blades. Landis was tried and acquitted of involuntary manslaughter, and Warner Bros. paid millions to settle lawsuits. Morrow, the star of *Combat!* from 1962 to 1967 on ABC-TV, left strong impressions in *The Glass House* (1972), *Police Story* (1973) and *Roots* (1977). He was fifty-three, Myca seven and Renee six.

JULY 24

1991—*COTTON CLUB* KILLERS CONVICTED

Eight years after the bullet-mutilated corpse of Broadway producer Roy Radin was found in a creek bed near Gorman, California, a Los Angeles Superior Court jury found cocaine dealer Karen "Laynie" Greenberger and three henchmen—all former bodyguards of *Hustler* magazine publisher Larry Flynt—guilty of murder and kidnapping on July 23, 1991. The crimes were related to the back-room financing conducted by Greenberger's former boyfriend, former Paramount Pictures head Robert Evans, to produce Francis Ford Coppola's extravagant *The Cotton Club*. Greenberger, forty-three, and Robert Lowe, forty-four, were convicted of second-degree murder and kidnapping, while William Mentzer, forty-two, and Alex Marti, thirty, were convicted of first-degree murder. Greenberger hired the trio because she thought Radin was squeezing her out of her producer's credit on the movie. This was their first full day of lifetimes in prison; the punishments carried no possibility of parole. *The Cotton Club*, a speakeasy epic, bombed at the box office.

JULY 25

2006—DRUNK DRIVING LESSON

The kid who sees dead people almost joined them on July 20, 2006, when he drove his 1995 Saturn into a mailbox that was situated on a brick base, flipping over the vehicle in the Los Angeles northern suburb of La Canada Flintridge. After the accident investigation by the Los Angeles County Sheriff's Department and a stay in Huntington Hospital in Pasadena, Haley Joel Osment nursed a broken rib, fractured right shoulder blade and cuts and abrasions on this date. On October 19, the star of *The Sixth Sense* (1999), *Pay It Forward* (2000) and *A.I.: Artificial Intelligence* (2001) pleaded no contest to misdemeanor counts of driving under the influence of alcohol and drug possession. Osment was sentenced to three years' probation, sixty hours in an alcohol rehab program, a fine of $1,500 and twenty-six Alcoholics Anonymous meetings.

JULY 26

1991—PEE-WEE HERMAN'S PEE-WEE HERMAN

While he visited relatives in Sarasota, Florida, Paul Reubens, aka Pee-wee Herman, geeky hero to kids everywhere, was arrested for masturbating in public in an adult movie theater. Sarasota detectives, on a periodic indecent-exposure sweep in the porn theater, caught him. The arrest was widely covered, and both Pee-wee and Reubens, star of the big-screen hits *Pee-wee's Big Adventure* (1985) and *Big Top Pee-wee* (1988), became personas non grata. CBS-TV stopped airing the extremely successful *Pee-wee's Playhouse*, and Disney-MGM Studios suspended from its studio tour a video that showed Pee-wee explaining how voice-over tracks were made. Toys "R" Us removed Pee-wee toys from its stores. Forgiving Hollywood invited Reubens back for *Batman Returns* (1992), *Mystery Men* (1999), *Blow* (2001) and TV roles.

JULY 27

1988—MURDER OF JUDITH BARSI

An in-demand child actress of the 1980s, Judith Barsi was on *Punky Brewster*, *Remington Steele* and other shows, in such movies as *Slam Dance* (1987) and *Jaws: The Revenge* (1987) and was a voice actress for Don Bluth's animation features *The Land Before Time* (1988) and, posthumously, *All Dogs Go to Heaven* (1989). Her father, Jozsef Barsi, and mother, Maria, had both escaped from Communist Hungary at different times and met in a Los Angeles restaurant. Judith was born on June 6, 1978. A plumbing contractor, Jozsef was arrested three times for drunk driving while Judith earned $100,000 during the fourth grade. She broke down in an audition and was seen by a psychologist, who reported Jozsef's severe mental and physical abuse to Child Protective Services. On July 25, 1988, Jozsef shot Judith to death while she slept in their Canoga Park home, bought with her earnings. When Maria entered the hall after hearing the gunshot, he murdered her, too. After two days with the corpses, he set them on fire on this date, walked into the garage with a .32-caliber pistol and blew his brains out. Judith was ten.

JULY 28

Mel Gibson was clocked by Malibu police going eighty-seven miles per hour in a forty-five-mile-per-hour zone on Pacific Coast Highway in his Lexus LS430 at 2:30 a.m. on this date. The cops arrested him for suspicion of drunk driving. Since it was his first DUI, he was released on $5,000 bail. However, Mr. Mel got a bit lippy at the booking, angrily telling the arresting officer, "Fucking Jews…the Jews are responsible for all the wars in the world." At various times, the American-born, Aussie-raised star of the *Mad Max* and *Lethal Weapon* franchises, as well as the Oscar-winning *Braveheart* (1995) and many movies, has been pigeonholed for bigotry versus gays, women or Jews. He has denied being anti-anything and apologized publicly for the tirade. On August 17, Gibson pleaded no contest to a misdemeanor DUI and was sentenced to three years' probation. He attended self-help meetings and a First Offenders Program, was fined $1,300 and his license was restricted.

JULY 29

1976—LIZ AND DICK: FINAL SPLITSVILLE

Elizabeth Taylor and Richard Burton remarried sixteen months after their initial divorce in 1974. In trying to make it work again, Burton remarked, "You can't keep clapping a couple of sticks [of dynamite] together without expecting them to blow up." The two-time Oscar-winning actress and Burton, a six-time nominee, had remarried in a private ceremony in Kasane, Botswana, but soon separated and re-divorced on this date. Their union has often been likened to a facsimile of their bitter repartee in Mike Nichols's film of Edward Albee's *Who's Afraid of Virginia Woolf?* (1966). Burton eventually received his seventh Oscar nomination, for *Equus* (1977), but never saw the gold during a career in which he received accolades as the greatest classical actor of his generation.

JULY 30

2007—Rebecca Schaeffer's Murderer Stabbed

Robert John Bardo, serving a life sentence for murdering actress Rebecca Schaeffer in July 1989, was recovering on this date after being stabbed eleven times on his way to breakfast on July 28, 2007. The perp was another inmate in Mule Creek State Prison in Amador County, California. As Bardo coagulated beneath his bandages, he could rest on his horrifically attained laurels—the knowledge that his stalking and brutal shooting of Schaeffer at her Los Angeles apartment had a national ripple effect. Bardo's killing led to California enacting Penal Code 646.9, the anti-stalking law, which then led to all fifty states and the District of Columbia enacting similar laws. Schaeffer, the rising star of the TV sitcom *My Sister Sam*, also had a role in Woody Allen's *Radio Days* (1989). She was preparing for an interview with director Francis Ford Coppola for a role in *The Godfather Part III* (1990) when she opened her door to Bardo's knock. She was twenty-one.

JULY 31

1995—WATERWORLD ALL WET

Costing more than $200 million to make, *Waterworld* was the most expensive movie made up to its time—a "gigantic money sponge," wrote James Robert Parish. Kevin Costner starred as a post-apocalyptic half-man, half-fish called the Mariner for director Kevin Reynolds. The Kevins had vacillated between camaraderie and contretemps through several projects, including *Robin Hood: Prince of Thieves* (1991) and *Rapa Nui* (1994). On *Waterworld*, stunt performers were exhausted by rough waters off Kawaihae, on the big island of Hawaii, where the sets, one thousand tons of steel, were built on the water. The main set sank once. Jellyfish stung the crew, whose unions claimed at least $2.7 million for labor violations. The scheduled 96-day shoot ballooned to 166 days. The production defied the tenet to never make an entire movie on the water. It defied common sense and took in $88 million domestically, or less than half what it cost to make.

AUGUST 1

1987—SEAN BEHIND BARS

Sean Penn began serving a court-ordered, two-month jail term on this date at a private facility in Bridgeport, California, as part of a punitive package including counseling and two years' probation for two parole violations in the previous six months. The violations were for assault on a movie extra, Jeffrey Klein, who attempted to photograph the actor on April 2 and was beaten by Penn after the two spit on each other; and for reckless and drunk driving after police pulled Penn over in May for speeding. He left the mountain retreat to briefly film a role in his father, Leo Penn's, movie *Judgment in Berlin* (1988). Back in Bridgeport, Sean got sick of hearing about his coddled treatment and had himself transferred to the Los Angeles County Jail, where the star of *Fast Times at Ridgemont High* (1982), *Racing with the Moon* (1984) and *At Close Range* (1986) filled a cell across the hall from the "Night Stalker," serial killer Richard Ramirez.

AUGUST 2

1957—"TRIAL OF 100 STARS"

Publisher Robert Harrison's scandal rag *Confidential* was sued for $1 million in May 1955 by Robert Mitchum and for $2 million in February 1957 by Dorothy Dandridge. Both suits claimed the sheet published false stories alleging public nudity: "Robert Mitchum—The Nude Who Came to Dinner" and "What Was Dorothy Dandridge Doing in the Woods?" Hollywood solidarity followed with an approach to Sacramento. A criminal libel and conspiracy lawsuit was filed on this date by California attorney general Edmund G. "Pat" Brown: *The People of the State of California v. Robert Harrison, et al.*

The star witness was former *Confidential* employee Howard Rushmore, who recalled fudging the truth and creating outright lies concerning Marilyn Monroe, Clark Gable, Frank Sinatra, Deanna Durbin, Tyrone Power and others. After two months of lurid testimony in the press-labeled "Trial of 100 Stars," the charges were dropped in October 1957 when Harrison agreed to cease publishing and pay out-of-court settlements for damages, $40,000 to Liberace and almost as much to a dozen others.

Liberace was a beneficiary of the "Trial of 100 Stars."

AUGUST 3

One of the most promising actors of his generation, Ray Sharkey was back in Los Angeles on this date after being fired in Vancouver, British Columbia, from the Stephen J. Cannell–produced series *The Hat Squad*. Ray had been arrested for possession of cocaine and heroin a few days earlier. He also faced something more difficult than his drug habit. The star of *Wiseguy* from 1987 to 1990 and costar of such movies as *Who'll Stop the Rain?* (1978), *Paradise Alley* (1978), *The Idolmaker* (1980) and *Wired* (1989) was HIV positive and knew it. He had infected his actress girlfriend, Elena Monica, the daughter of comedian Corbett Monica. She eventually sued Ray for $52 million for infecting her with the virus that causes AIDS. She won the case, but he had so little money at the end that she received nothing. Ray Sharkey died of AIDS on June 11, 1993, in the Lutheran Medical Center in Brooklyn, New York. He was forty.

AUGUST 4

1967—*BONNIE AND CLYDE* ARRIVES

The Montreal Film Festival provided the launching pad on this date for a new brand of cinema, one of amoral immediacy that tapped into a generation changing in fast and violent modes from Vietnam, civil rights, political assassinations and the drug culture. The picture pushed the envelope of violence portrayed on the screen with bloody shootings, especially in the culminating massacre of the title duo, based on notable bank robbers of the 1930s. Director Arthur Penn and producer-star Warren Beatty's film was met with critical confusion by critics and patrons. *Newsweek*'s Joe Morgenstern called the film a "squalid shoot-'em-up for the moron trade" on August 21 and reversed his opinion a week later, noting scene after scene of dazzling artistry. The film created new stars in Faye Dunaway and Gene Hackman, affirmed Beatty's place as a top star and conferred a master's status on Penn.

AUGUST 5

1962—MARILYN: HORIZONTAL FOREVER

The all-time blonde bombshell was found dead on this date in the bedroom of her Brentwood home by psychiatrist Ralph Greenson. Monroe's housekeeper called him, suspecting the worst behind the actress's locked bedroom door. The cause of death was determined by the Los Angeles County coroner's office to be "acute barbiturate poisoning" and was listed as "probable suicide." Then and in the intervening half century since her death, Marilyn's passing has been the subject of perhaps as much speculation as the Kennedy assassinations, and many believe her to have been murdered, including at least one LAPD officer at the scene. No murder charges were ever filed. The former wife of baseball icon Joe DiMaggio and playwright Arthur Miller, Marilyn was known to abuse narcotics. Conspiracy theories and investigations way after the fact have dragged in speculation on the Kennedys, Frank Sinatra and others. Marilyn was thirty-six.

AUGUST 6

1965—MERCURIAL PLAYER GOES DARK

Beaky and often in specs, Everett Sloane entered movies as one of Orson Welles's Mercury Theatre players in *Citizen Kane* (1941) and became a sought-after character actor. Sloane also acted with boy-genius impresario Welles in *Journey into Fear* (1942), *Lady from Shanghai* (1946) and *Prince of Foxes* (1949) and with Marlon Brando in *The Men* (1950), Kirk Douglas in *Lust for Life* (1956) and Paul Newman in *Somebody Up There Likes Me* (1956). Ubiquitous on television, Sloane is probably best remembered as the ruthless businessman in the film version of Rod Serling's *Patterns* (1956) and as the small-town father of a girl pregnant out of wedlock who shoots Robert Mitchum and then himself in *Home from the Hill* (1960). Despondent over his advanced glaucoma and the inevitable coming blindness, Sloane took his own life on this date with sleeping pills. He was fifty-five.

AUGUST 7

1995—BEGELMAN: END OF THE AFFAIR

Former Columbia Pictures president David Begelman shot himself on this date in the Century Plaza Hotel in Century City. Begelman started Creative Management Associates (CMA), which pioneered the "packaging" of stars, writers and directors from the agency in film projects. He then ran Columbia, presiding over the making of Warren Beatty's *Shampoo* (1975) and Steven Spielberg's *Close Encounters of the Third Kind* (1978). But he fell from power in 1977 when he was accused of forging checks, including in the names of Cliff Robertson and director Martin Ritt, and the misappropriation of funds. He was eventually convicted of grand theft, but the charge was reduced from a felony to a misdemeanor in 1979, when he was hired to run MGM's motion picture division. After getting fired from that, he became a producer. The Columbia scandal became the subject of David McClintick's 1982 bestseller *Indecent Exposure*. Begelman was seventy-three.

AUGUST 8

On location in Gila Bend, Arizona, during filming on *The Man Who Loved Cat Dancing*, Sarah Miles's assistant, David Whiting, was found dead in the star's hotel room. She was initially a person of interest, but the death was ruled a suicide. This wasn't before all sorts of gossip flew, including the rumor that Miles and costar Burt Reynolds were conducting an affair, somewhat mirroring their movie's plot of his outlaw abducting her and the two becoming lovers. She was married to Oscar-winning screenwriter Robert Bolt, and Reynolds was dating talk-show host Dinah Shore. No affair was ever proven as part of the location melodrama, portrayed this month in "A Corpse as Big as the Ritz" by Ron Rosenbaum in *Esquire*. The film, which costarred George Hamilton and Lee J. Cobb, was generally judged as a standard western.

AUGUST 9

1969—"HELTER SKELTER" MURDERS

Five bloody corpses were discovered on this date at 10050 Cielo Drive, Beverly Hills, the home of director Roman Polanski and his wife, actress Sharon Tate. Charles Manson's cult "family" shot eighteen-year-old Steve Parent, who drove near the scene where the pregnant Tate, hair stylist Jay Sebring, screenwriter Wojciech Frykowski and coffee fortune heiress Abigail Folger were stabbed to death. Polanski was in Europe. The following day, Rosemary and Leno LaBianca were discovered stabbed to death in their Waverly Drive home in Los Angeles. Manson had once attended a party next door so, crackpot-killer logic being what it is, figured he couldn't be traced to 3301 Waverly Drive, the LaBianca home. Prior to the Tate murders, 10050 Cielo had been Henry Fonda's home and was the honeymoon nest in 1965 for Cary Grant and Dyan Cannon. Buyers razed the structure in 1994, built a Mediterranean villa and renumbered the property to 10066 Cielo Drive.

AUGUST 10

1984—MPAA: EXPLORE MORE GORE

Director John Milius's *Red Dawn* became on this date the first film released with a PG-13 rating. In 1984, parents and parental groups protested the gore and violence in *Indiana Jones and the Temple of Doom* and *Gremlins*, both of which were rated PG. These complaints prodded Steven Spielberg, director of *Temple of Doom* and producer of *Gremlins*, to suggest a new rating to Motion Picture Association of America president Jack Valenti for movies that have excessive adult content over and above a PG rating but not enough to rate an R or "restricted" designation. Valenti's talks with cinema chain owners led to the introduction of the PG-13 rating on July 1, 1984. PG-13 indicated that some material may be inappropriate for children under thirteen. *Dreamscape* and *The Woman in Red* were released the following week. *The Flamingo Kid* was the first picture labeled PG-13 but was not released until December 1984.

AUGUST 11

1981—PALIMONY SHMALIMONY: THE MARVIN CASE

The California Court of Appeals ruled in *Marvin v. Marvin* on this date that Michelle Triola Marvin was not entitled to half of Lee Marvin's earnings from 1964 through 1970, ending a six-year legal tangle and warding off a frighteningly poised alliance of gold diggers and attorneys. In 1976, nightclub singer Michelle's attorney contended she was entitled to half of the approximately $3.6 million that Lee earned in those years, plus $100,000 for the loss of her career. This high-profile "palimony" suit was followed closely by the press since more couples were foregoing marriage. A box-office star in that period, Marvin had fronted *Cat Ballou* (1965), *The Professionals* (1966), *The Dirty Dozen* (1967) and *Point Blank* (1968). He prevailed on appeal when the appellate court ruled that "adults who voluntarily live together and engage in sexual relations are nonetheless as competent as any other persons to contract respecting their earnings and property rights." Michelle received $104,000 from the actor for rehab.

AUGUST 12

1988—Blasphemous Portrayal of Christ

The Last Temptation of Christ, director Martin Scorsese's interpretation of a screenplay by Paul Schrader, went into limited U.S. release on this date and became the most controversial movie in years. The title temptation by Satan is portrayed as an alternative reality in which Christ marries Mary Magdalene and lives a mortal life, learns of the satanic deception and ends up back on the cross. Willem Dafoe portrayed Jesus, who consummates marriage with Mary Magdalene, kisses men, regrets his sins and is involved in other transgressions from the Gospel. Boycotts were threatened. Releasing studio Universal's parent corporation, MCA, was picketed. The General Cinemas chain refused to exhibit the movie. A Paris theater showing the picture was firebombed. Several countries banned the film. Generally well reviewed, the film garnered only one Oscar nomination, for Scorsese for best director.

AUGUST 13

1965—*Faster, Pussycat! Kill! Kill!*

Producer-director Russ Meyer's singular brand of voluptuous-babe, crazy-crime cinema went mainstream with *Beyond the Valley of the Dolls* (1970). But the enduring masterwork for Meyer cultists is *Faster, Pussycat! Kill! Kill!*, which ended its first week of release on this date. The plot follows three hyper-sexed go-go girls in the Mojave Desert who kidnap a couple, kill the boyfriend and try to rip off a crippled gas station owner. An enduring fascination of the film, which is absent nudity, is its status as the career apex of Tura Satana, playing vicious ringleader Varla. Japanese-born Tura entered the United States with a fake ID at age thirteen, turned down Elvis Presley's marriage proposal and became a character actress (on *Hawaiian Eye*, *The Man from UNCLE*, etc.), nude model and touring exotic dancer. She eventually became an LAPD dispatcher and married a police officer. She died of heart failure on February 4, 2011, in Reno, Nevada. Tura was seventy-two.

AUGUST 14

1980—TRAGEDY OF DOROTHY STRATTEN

Actress and former *Playboy* model Dorothy Stratten was murdered on this date by Paul Snider, who had married her in Vancouver, British Columbia, before both came to Hollywood. He killed her with a shotgun, abused the corpse and then killed himself. She had become the magazine's Playmate of the Year and seemed destined for movie stardom after surviving *Skatetown U.S.A.* (1979) and the sci-fi send-up *Galaxina* (1980) by costarring with Audrey Hepburn and Ben Gazzara in director Peter Bogdanovich's *They All Laughed* (1981). The events of her final months were portrayed in director Bob Fosse's *Star 80* (1983), with Mariel Hemingway as Dorothy, Eric Roberts as Snider and Cliff Robertson as *Playboy* publisher Hugh Hefner. Stratten had begun an affair with Bogdanovich, and Snider hired a private eye to tail her. Intending to file for divorce, Stratten moved in with Bogdanovich. By August 1980, Snider correctly believed he had lost his "rocket to the moon." She was twenty.

AUGUST 15

Pioneering aviator and barnstormer Wiley Post sought an air route from the West Coast to Russia. His fellow Oklahoman, the Native American former cowboy and vaudevillian, humorist and movie star Will Rogers, sought material for his syndicated column. Post's northwest adventure seemed fertile column material. They left Seattle in early August and, on this date, ascended out of Fairbanks, Alaska, bound for Point Barrow. Uncertain of their position in bad weather, Post landed in a lagoon to ask directions. On takeoff, the engine failed at low altitude, and the nose-heavy aircraft, uncontrollable at low speed, plunged into the lagoon, shearing off the right wing and ending inverted in shallow water. Both men were killed instantly. Rogers, one of America's most recognizable personalities, had made seventy-one pictures, including the popular *Doctor Bull* (1933), *Judge Priest* (1934) and *Steamboat Round the Bend* (1935) for director John Ford. Rogers and Post were eulogized across America for a week. Rogers was fifty-five, Post thirty-six.

AUGUST 16

Elvis supposedly died on this date on the bathroom floor at his Graceland mansion in Memphis. Found by his road manager, the Tupelo, Mississippi son was rushed to Baptist Memorial Hospital in Memphis, where he was pronounced dead. The Shelby County, Tennessee coroner recorded the cause of death as cardiac arrhythmia—the heart beat irregularly and finally stopped. The attending physicians deliberately omitted the fact that the cause of the stopped heart was an overdose of prescription drugs. These drugs included codeine, Valium, morphine and Demerol. Elvis's favorite sandwich, deep-fried bacon and peanut butter, didn't help. After the drug information was revealed, Vernon Presley, Elvis's father, had the autopsy sealed, and it will remain so until 2027, or fifty years after the King's death. Elvis is supposedly buried at Graceland, but he occasionally is sighted here and there, sometimes in Vegas. The King was supposedly forty-two.

AUGUST 17

2011—BULLETIN: JACKIE CHAN IS ALIVE

Rumors that stunt-happy martial artist and action star Jackie Chan was dead ran rampant on Twitter on this date. The social networking site, which has promulgated other rumors of celeb demises, sent concerned users hunting down reports of Jackie's death. The celebrity death hoax spread across boundaries to Facebook, where an "R.I.P. Jackie Chan" community cropped up, logging eighty-two thousand "likes." The problem with all of this is that Jackie, no stranger to death-defying feats, owns four production companies, a theater chain, clothing line, Jackie's Kitchen restaurant chain and other businesses and is an ambassador for UNICEF and a supporter of Save China's Tigers, Jackie Chan Charitable Foundation and Dragon's Heart Foundation, bringing help to children and the elderly in remote portions of China. He's been too busy to die.

AUGUST 18

1956—BELA LUGOSI RETURNS TO THE COFFIN

The greatest screen vampire of them all was buried on this date in Holy Cross Cemetery in Culver City, California, the victim of a heart attack, sans any use of a wooden stake. During the viewing at Utter-McKinley Mortuary on Hollywood Boulevard, Peter Lorre supposedly addressed the corpse, which was prone in the sort of casket out of which Bela, in *Dracula* (1931) and other films, rose many times on

the screen. Lorre supposedly urged, "Come on, Bela, you're putting us on!" Lugosi died on August 16 during production on director Ed Wood's *Plan 9 from Outer Space*. Often cited as the worst feature film ever made, *Plan 9* was released three years after Bela died; the filmmaker's wife's chiropractor, with a cape over his face, completed Lugosi's limited role. These incidents, as well as Lugosi's narcotics addiction and late-career penury, were portrayed in director Tim Burton's *Ed Wood* (1993), with Martin Landau in his Oscar-winning role as Bela.

AUGUST 19

1979—BRANDO: BULKED-UP BUDDHA

Francis Ford Coppola's Vietnam War epic *Apocalypse Now*, in its first week of release on this date, concerned a U.S. Army officer's mission to assassinate a former U.S. Special Forces officer who becomes a jungle potentate in Cambodia. Coppola hired the fifty-two-year-old Marlon Brando as the quarry, Colonel Kurtz, and the actor promised to lose weight to portray a former Green Beret. But the five-foot, ten-inch Brando showed up on location in the Philippines at more than 235 pounds. Cinematographer Vittorio Storaro shot Brando's scenes in shadow, and the actor wore a monk-like smock to hide his girth, improvising a stream-of-consciousness dialogue. Coppola refused for the Buddha-like Brando to be another setback. Sets had

been wiped out by a typhoon, lead actor Harvey Keitel was exchanged for Martin Sheen and the helicopters operated at the whim of the Filipino government. The film was nominated for eight Oscars, including best picture, and won two, for Storaro's cinematography and the sound.

Marlon Brando (right) was the quarry of Martin Sheen's assassin in Francis Ford Coppola's *Apocalypse Now* (1979).

AUGUST 20

1947—GRABLE'S MILLION-DOLLAR GAMS

Mother Wore Tights, the signature picture of Betty Grable's career, was released on this date in New York City, when she was the highest paid woman in America, earning $300,000 from Twentieth Century-Fox, and the studio insured her legs for $1 million each with Lloyd's of London. Grable's photograph became the No. 1 pin-up image for servicemen during World War II. A top box-office draw, Elizabeth Ruth Grable of St. Louis, Missouri, displayed a talent for hoofing in frothy escapades: *The Shocking Miss Pilgrim* (1947), *That Lady in Ermine* (1947), *The Beautiful Blonde from Bashful Bend* (1949) and *How to Marry a Millionaire* (1953). Grable divorced former child actor Jackie Coogan and bandleader Harry James before cohabitating with Bob Remick for her remaining twenty-two years. She died of cancer in 1973 in Santa Monica. Betty was fifty-six.

AUGUST 21

1938—BOGIE, HOLD THE MAYO NEXT TIME

Mayo Methot, a tempestuous, hard-drinking former Broadway actress, married rising Warner Bros. tough-guy star Humphrey Bogart on this date, beginning what screenwriter Julius J. Epstein called the "sequel to the Civil War." The battles included her chasing girls away from Bogie with a broken pop bottle and then chasing Bogie with it. Once, as guests arrived at the Bogarts', Mayo barricaded herself in an upstairs room with a revolver. Another time, she settled the discussion over who was going to carve the turkey by heaving it out a window. She stabbed him with a knife; he affectionately called her "Sluggy." Bogie, forty-four, wrangled out of this jam, obtaining a divorce in 1945 and marrying a teenager, nineteen-year-old Lauren Bacall, his costar in *To Have and Have Not* (1945). The nuptials were on May 21, 1945, on the farm of Bogie's pal, Pulitzer Prize–winning conservationist author Louis Bromfield, near Lucas, Ohio. Mayo died in Multnomah, Oregon, on June 9, 1951. She was forty-seven.

Humphrey Bogart (far right) starred in *Casablanca* (1942) with (from left) Paul Henreid, Ingrid Bergman and Claude Rains.

AUGUST 22

1927—CHAPLIN'S MEDIA CIRCUS

Lita Grey was sixteen and Charlie Chaplin thirty-five when she allegedly became pregnant in 1924. They secretly married in Empalme, Sonora, Mexico, skirting any charge of sexual relations with a minor. But the scandal was only postponed while he finished *The Gold Rush* (1925) and prepared *The Circus* (1928). After they had two children, Charles Jr. in 1925 and Sydney Earle in 1926, the fur flew

in a sensational divorce. Official on this date, the split was based on Lita's lengthy complaint featuring the then-scandalous claims of Chaplin's sexual affairs with multiple women. Charlie was ordered to pay Lita $625,000 and to establish $100,000 trust funds for each child. It was the largest divorce settlement up to that time. Lita married three more times, clerked in Robinson's Department Store in Beverly Hills and wrote two autobiographies, *My Life with Chaplin* (1966) and *The Wife of the Life of the Party* (1995). She died in 1995 at age eighty-seven.

AUGUST 23

1926—VALENTINO: MORTIFIED AND PETRIFIED

The heartthrob's demise on this date at the height of his fame was from peritonitis after an operation for a perforated ulcer and appendicitis. The thirty-one-year-old former ballroom dancer and star of *The Sheik* (1921) and *Blood and Sand* (1922) was born Rodolfo Guglielmi and linked romantically with screen stars Nazimova and Pola Negri. Women swooned over his swarthy looks, while journalist Adela Rogers St. Johns characterized his effect on American men: their wives could fantasize about Clark Gable, the kind of guy they would like to be, but they resented Valentino, an interloping foreigner, a gigolo. Newspapermen portrayed him as effete, and the son of Italy suffered much indignation. An estimated 100,000 people lined New York City's streets to pay their respects at the Frank E. Campbell Funeral Home.

AUGUST 24

1995—BING'S BOYS

Gary Crosby died from lung cancer on this date in Burbank, California. He was sixty-two. A semi-regular on *Dragnet*, Crosby also sang in the footsteps of his father, recording legend, Oscar-winning actor and radio and TV personality Harry Lillis "Bing" Crosby. Gary's autobiography, *Going My Own Way*, was published in 1983. This shocker detailed Bing's mental and physical abuse of sons Gary, Philip, Lindsay

and Dennis, fostered with his first wife, singer Dixie Lee. Casually puffing on a pipe, Bing usually was seen as a cardigan-clad every-dad with a song in his heart and a wisecrack for Bob Hope. In such films as *Going My Way* (1944) and *White Christmas* (1954), Bing was fatherly in a variety of ways. At home, self-confessed alcoholic Gary contended, Bing was a monster to be feared. Philip Crosby stuck up for dad, but Lindsay and Dennis both committed suicide by shotgun blast, in 1989 and 1991, respectively. Philip married four times, thrice to Las Vegas showgirls, and then died in 2004 of a heart attack at age sixty-nine.

AUGUST 25

1989—WOODS V. YOUNG

In one of the messier affairs in Hollywood annals, James Woods and Sean Young, costars of the drug-addiction film *The Boost* (1988), were the alleged male victim and female terrorist in a real-life episode of *Fatal Attraction*. Woods's $6 million harassment lawsuit against the actress, charging "intentional infliction of emotional distress," was announced settled on this date, without any particulars. After an alleged affair on the *Boost* set, he dumped her to return to his fiancée. Woods's mail thereafter contained hate notes and pictures of corpses and dismembered animals. A mutilated doll was found at his door. Young denied the suit's accusations to police and FBI investigators and denied any affair with the Oscar nominee for *Salvador* (1986). Both actors have kept busy, Young in small roles in small pictures and Woods in *Nixon* (1995), *Ghosts of Mississippi* (1996) and other films and TV productions. He has earned eight Emmy nominations (and two wins for *Hallmark Hall of Fame* presentations).

AUGUST 26

1961—BOTTLE CLAIMS ANOTHER

A doe-eyed actress from Chicago who had made an impact in such films as *Our Hearts Were Young and Gay* (1944) and *Night Has a Thousand Eyes* (1948), Gail Russell starred opposite John Wayne in *Angel and the Badman* (1947) and *Wake of the Red Witch* (1948). Extremely shy, she retreated into alcohol to calm her stage fright, and in 1949, she married actor Guy Madison. Paramount didn't renew her contract, specifically because of her drinking, and she and Madison divorced. The Duke, who created Batjac Productions, remained loyal and hired her after a five-year absence to costar with Randolph Scott and Lee Marvin in director Budd Boetticher's *Seven Men from Now* (1956).

A problem occurred when, during a visit to Jan's Coffee Shop on Beverly Boulevard in Los Angeles, Gail drove her convertible inside the café. She failed a sobriety test, and unflattering pictures made the papers. Russell was found dead in her Brentwood apartment on this date, the victim of liver damage and malnutrition. She was thirty-six.

AUGUST 27

1978—EARLY TRIP TO THE BEYOND

Longtime character actor and novelist/playwright Robert Shaw had finally made it to the front rank of Hollywood's bankable stars when he died suddenly of cardiac arrest on this date. He was fifty-one. He had menaced James Bond in *Dr. No* (1962), commanded the Nazis in *Battle of the Bulge* (1965), received an Oscar nomination for *A Man for All Seasons* (1966), was famously ripped off in *The Sting* (1973), became the most memorable human appetizer in *Jaws* (1975), wrote *The Man in the Glass Booth* (1975) and fronted such pictures as *The Taking of Pelham One Two Three* (1974) and *The Deep* (1976). The father of ten from three marriages, Shaw was often the picture of virility. His death shocked filmgoers who saw him running through Super Bowl stands in John Frankenheimer's *Black Sunday* (1977). An engraved stone in Tourmakeady, County Mayo, Ireland, where he lived and died, commemorates his passing.

AUGUST 28

1951—WALKER TO THE MAKER

Robert Walker had been an expressive presence in memorable films: *Madame Curie* (1943), *Thirty Seconds Over Tokyo* (1945) and *One Touch of Venus* (1948). His first marriage to Jennifer Jones ended when she took up with producer David O. Selznick, who forced them to do take after take of a love scene in *Since You Went Away* (1944). Walker was treated in 1949 at the Menninger Clinic in Topeka, Kansas, for psychosis and was cast in his most famous part, as Bruno the scheming killer, with Farley Granger in Alfred Hitchcock's *Strangers on a Train* (1951). Walker's final film was *My Son John* (1952). He died before production finished, and shots of his death scene in *Strangers on a Train* were spliced into *My Son John*. Walker's housekeeper found the actor boozy and distressed on this date and called a psychiatrist, who sedated him with amobarbital. Walker passed out and stopped breathing. Resuscitation failed. The combination of the alcohol and drug was suspected to have killed him. He was thirty-two.

AUGUST 29

1978—JOINING HIS BELOVED

Frenchmen Charles Boyer and Maurice Chevalier alternated as the epitome in European sophistication in American pictures. Boyer's deep accent and courtly manner charmed America opposite Greta Garbo, Marlene Dietrich, Jean Harlow, Jean Arthur, Bette Davis, Ingrid Bergman and many others. But Boyer was charmed himself by B-movie starlet Pat Paterson, who retired after her only "A" picture, *Idiot's Delight* (1940). Boyer married Paterson in 1934 and remained dedicated to her the remainder of her life, which ended from cancer on August 24, 1978. Their son, Michael, had taken his own life on September 22, 1965, playing Russian roulette with a revolver after a girlfriend left him. Two days after his wife's death and two shy of his seventy-ninth birthday, Chuck decided to join her via an overdose of Seconal. All three Boyers are buried at Holy Cross Cemetery in Culver City, California.

AUGUST 30

1979—SEBERG DEAD IN PARIS

A native of Marshalltown, Iowa, Jean Seberg was "discovered" by director Otto Preminger to portray Joan of Arc in the lavish box-office dud *Saint Joan* (1957). She gained notoriety in Jean-Luc Godard's *Breathless* (1960) and opposite Warren Beatty in *Lilith* (1964) and attained U.S. stardom in *Paint Your Wagon* (1969), *Pendulum* (1969) and *Airport* (1970). But her publicized connection to the Black Panther movement and the 1970 death of her infant, Nina, attributable to her own overdose on sleeping pills during pregnancy, made her a pariah. She relocated to Europe, racked up three marriages and attempted suicide on several of Nina's posthumous birthdays. Eleven days after being reported missing, her lifeless body was found on this date in the back seat of her car, parked near her apartment. Parisian police stated she had overdosed on barbiturates and alcohol. A suicide note read, "Forgive me. I can no longer live with my nerves." The Paris coroner left the cause at "probable suicide." She was forty.

AUGUST 31

1948—BIG BAD BOB BUSTED

In Hollywood's first big postwar scandal, film noir icon Robert Mitchum went down for possession of marijuana and conspiracy. The cigs were crammed into his palm as the cops came through the door at a Laurel Canyon bungalow, where he had been lured by mob-connected bartender Robin Ford with actress Lila Leeds and dancer Vicki Evans. Mitchum served three months at Wayside Honor Farm, which he called "Palm Springs without the riff-raff." The star of *The Story of G.I. Joe* (1945) and *Out of the Past* (1947) didn't fight the phony conviction to appear "bought off." But the conviction was expunged from the record in 1950 when the Los Angeles County district attorney learned that Mitchum had been framed. Mitchum's stardom endured for more than half a century through such classics as *The Night of the Hunter* (1955), *Heaven Knows, Mr. Allison* (1957) and *The Sundowners* (1960), as well as the epic miniseries *Winds of War* (1983) and *War and Remembrance* (1988–89). He died in 1997 at age seventy-nine.

SEPTEMBER 1

1955—FRANK AND JOE'S EXCELLENT ADVENTURE

Frank Sinatra and Joe DiMaggio were having dinner on November 5, 1954, at Frank's favorite Hollywood joint, Villa Capri, when Joltin' Joe's private eye reported that Joe's recently divorced (on October 27, 1954) wife, Marilyn Monroe, had just ducked into a nearby love nest with her vocal coach. The disgraced Yankee Clipper, fired-up Frank, Villa Capri maitre d' Billy Karen and pro peepers Barney Ruditsky and Phil Irwin barged over to the tryst site. This well-oiled crew, about three bricks shy of an *Ocean's Eleven* load, kicked down the door to photograph Marilyn *in flagrante delicto*. Instead, they found Florence Kotz screaming at the breaking and entering by America's two most iconic Italian Americans. Oops! Another Drinking with Frank 101 field trip would have stayed just that, except *Confidential* unleashed the story in its September 1955 issue. A libel trial against the scandal rag brought the "Wrong Door Raid" up again in 1958, the same year Kotz settled her lawsuit for $7,500. Marilyn, who was ensconced in the upstairs apartment, was divorced at the time, so any photos would have had no currency.

SEPTEMBER 2

1940—LARRY AND VIV DUMP SPOUSES

His hits included *Wuthering Heights* (1939) and Alfred Hitchcock's *Rebecca* (1940). She basked in the glow of the Oscar for her Scarlett O'Hara in *Gone with the Wind* (1939). So, riding high and mighty, Laurence Olivier and Vivien Leigh dumped their albatrosses, consummated the inevitable and spent the third and final day of their honeymoon on Catalina Island on this date. Actress Jill Esmond had divorced the future Sir Larry (who became the Lord Olivier), and Barrister Herbert Leigh Holman finally agreed to divorce Leigh. The custody of Larry's

son Tarquin and Viv's daughter Suzanne went to the not-so-famous parents. On August 31, 1940, Olivier and Leigh were married at Ronald Colman's San Ysidro Ranch in the Montecito section of Santa Barbara, in a ceremony attended only by their witnesses, writer Garson Kanin and Katharine Hepburn, both of whom had been spirited up the coast in the middle of the night for the impromptu occasion. The Oliviers reigned as Hollywood's imported scandalous royalty into the 1950s.

SEPTEMBER 3

1952—DUKE AND MARSHAL MATT V. COMMIES

In Hollywood's most addled cold war concoction, *Big Jim McLain*, in its first week of release on this date, John Wayne and James Arness play House Un-American Activities Committee investigators ferreting out dirty Commies in the Hawaiian labor rackets. Held out of distribution for generations because of its wrongheaded politics— supporting the governmental blight of HUAC—the film was in the service of the Duke's politics through his Wayne-Fellows Productions (later Batjac). The Senator Joseph McCarthy–inspired HUAC assassinated careers with accusations of Commie ties, including in the film business, in which the "Hollywood Ten" and others were blackballed. In the film's courtroom opening, the six-foot, six-inch Arness rises in trembling anger when a Commie invokes his Fifth Amendment right to not incriminate himself. The Duke, grinning and reining in the future Marshal Matt Dillon like a Doberman handler, endorsed HUAC's abrogation of basic American rights. The picture is one of a kind.

SEPTEMBER 4

1993—DE FINAL PLANE TO DE SKY

Hervé Villechaize, the three-foot, eleven-inch actor who played Tattoo, Ricardo Montalban's sidekick, on the ABC-TV series *Fantasy Island* from 1977 to 1983, shot himself on this date on the backyard patio of his home on West Killian Street in North Hollywood. His common-law wife, Kathy Self, found him. He was rushed to the Medical Center of North Hollywood, where he died. The son of a Parisian surgeon, Hervé was fired off the series in its next-to-final season when he demanded as much money as anchoring star Montalban. Without Herve, the Spelling-Goldberg series failed in the ratings and was cancelled. Villechaize, who acted in *Greaser's Palace* (1972), *The Man with the Golden Gun* (1974), *Airplane II: The Sequel* (1982) and others, had contended with health problems in his final year from alcoholism, including pneumonia. He was cremated, and his ashes were scattered off Point Fermin in San Pedro. He was fifty.

SEPTEMBER 5

1932—PAUL BERN'S "SUICIDE"

Blonde bombshell Jean Harlow didn't have a second husband for long—from July 2, 1932, until this date. Her two-month hubby, Paul Bern, an MGM contract writer and director, was found shot to death in their Beverly Hills home. His "suicide note" has been called a forgery and was penned perhaps weeks before as an apology for sexual dysfunction. Harlow never spoke about the killing and famously kicked the bucket in 1937. Hollywood legend claims that Louis B. Mayer, Irving Thalberg and MGM's "fixer," Eddie Mannix, went to work on the murder scene before the LAPD got there to spin the suicide angle. In 1960, LA County district attorney William McKesson reopened the investigation and got nowhere. Ben Hecht and Sam Marx both have written that Bern's abandoned former common-law wife, Dorothy Millette, shot him. She committed suicide the next day by jumping overboard from the *Delta King* into the Sacramento River. Bern was forty-two, Millette probably forty-six.

SEPTEMBER 6

1994—HERE'S A KNIFE IN YOUR EYE!

During production on *Cyborg* (1989) in Wilmington, North Carolina, Jackson Pinckney, playing a pirate, lost his left eye when Jean-Claude Van Damme accidentally poked him in the peepers with a prop knife. Pinckney sued Van Damme and was awarded $485,000 by a North Carolina appellate court on this date. The eye-gouging scene allegedly made it into the final cut of director Albert Pyun's movie. The judge found that Van Damme engaged in "excessive contact" with the rubber prop knife. Pinckney, a Fort Bragg, North Carolina–based soldier, was medically discharged from the army because of the permanent partial blindness. Van Damme, a Belgian-born kickboxing champion with an obsession for performing weird cheerleader splits, was the second-division Arnold Schwarzenegger of his day and sought fight scenes with an authentic look. The judge ruled that his "reputation for engaging in excessive contact in order to do so" resulted in the authentic "look" that Pinckney's vision would forever have.

SEPTEMBER 7

1951—"CARIBBEAN CYCLONE" DROWNS

One of the World War II–era screen's "exotic beauties," Maria Antonia Garcia Vidal de Santo Silas (some sources insert "Africa" before or instead of Antonia), was born at Barahona, Dominican Republic, on June 6, 1912, and was one of the screen sirens who never made it past age thirty-nine. Swarthy, shapely, expressive, Maria Montez was known as the "Caribbean Cyclone," and her titles ran toward the exotic: *That Night in Rio* (1941), *South of Tahiti* (1941), *Arabian Nights* (1942), *White Savage* (1943), *Cobra Woman* (1944), *Gypsy Wildcat* (1944), etc. Her second husband was Jean-Pierre Aumont, a French freedom fighter during World War II and an actor thereafter. She moved to Paris to be with him after the war, and they had a child, Tina Aumont. On this date, Maria was found dead in her bathtub in Paris by her sisters, Ada and Teresita. Maria apparently drowned after a heart attack. No autopsy was performed. In 1996, the airport in Barahona was named the Maria Montez International Airport.

SEPTEMBER 8

1965—SO LONG, DOROTHY DANDRIDGE

She was the first African American woman to be nominated for the Academy Award for best actress, for Otto Preminger's *Carmen Jones* (1954). She also was the first black woman to appear on the cover of *Life* magazine. The body of this mesmerizing racial pioneer was found on this date by her manager, Earl Mills, on the bathroom floor of her Sunset Strip apartment. She was expected to fly to New York the next day for a nightclub engagement. A Los Angeles pathology institute determined the death was accidental, from an overdose of antidepressants. But the Los Angeles County coroner reported that "Miss Dandridge died of a rare embolism—blockage of the blood passages at the lungs and brain by tiny pieces of fat flaking off from bone marrow in a fractured right foot she sustained days before she died." A consort of Preminger and Peter Lawford, she had been married to dancer Harold Nicholas. Halle Berry won an Emmy Award portraying Dorothy in *Introducing Dorothy Dandridge* (1999). Dorothy was forty-two.

SEPTEMBER 9

1921—FATTY ARBUCKLE'S "HORSEPLAY"

At a party held on Labor Day, September 5, 1921, in the St. Francis Hotel in San Francisco, New York actress Virginia Rappe allegedly suffered physical trauma from horseplay with Arbuckle. She died on this date from a ruptured bladder and peritonitis. She had suffered from cystitis and previously from venereal disease and was a big drinker in spite of the sickness it caused her. No one at the three-suite soiree witnessed the "horseplay," but a woman rounded up for the party, Maude Delmont, accused Arbuckle in the death. Arbuckle was vigorously prosecuted by San Francisco district attorney Matthew Brady through three manslaughter trials blanketed by sensational newspaper coverage. Deadlocked juries in 1921 and early 1922 led to Fatty's acquittal on April 12, 1922, when the third jury deliberated for six minutes. Out $700,000 for legal fees and blackballed out of the business, Fatty hit the bottle. When he crawled out of it and signed a Warner Bros. contract on June 29, 1933, Fatty proclaimed it the "best day of my life." He promptly died that night in his sleep of a heart attack. He was forty-six.

SEPTEMBER 10

1958—LIZ STEALS EDDIE FISHER

Elizabeth Taylor was widowed on March 22, 1958, when her third husband, producer Mike Todd, died in the crash of his plane, *Lucky Liz*, in Cibola County, New Mexico. Rushing to Liz's grieving side were Eddie Fisher and Debbie Reynolds, married since 1955. Eddie stayed very cozy through his extremely public dumping of all-American sweetheart Debbie. On this date, Liz issued a statement through her publicist: "Eddie is not in love with Debbie and never has been." NBC-TV, aghast at the Liz-and-Eddie affair, cancelled *The Eddie Fisher Show*. Debbie took the high road: "I love my kids," including Carrie Fisher, the future Princess Leia in the *Star Wars* franchise. Liz's predatory

vamp status was solidified by art, such as it is, in *Butterfield 8* (1960), costarring with Eddie for her first Oscar win. As a John O'Hara–style pass-around package, she declares, "Mama, face it, I was the slut of all time!" Eddie, an el-lusho of the first water, was Liz's fourth notch (1959 to 1964), dumped for an even bigger alkie, Richard Burton.

SEPTEMBER 11

1920—"IDEAL GIRL" OLIVE THOMAS

Selznick Pictures received word from Paris on September 10, 1920, that the company's top star, Olive Thomas, had confused a glass of mercury bichloride for booze, downed it in her room at the Ritz and died from the poisoning in a Parisian hospital. The liquid actually was an external medication for the syphilis suffered by her husband, actor and cocaine addict Jack Pickford, brother of megastar Mary Pickford. Olive's stomach was pumped to no avail. The news broke in the United States on this date that the "Ideal American Girl" was dead. The former Oliveretta Elaine Duffy from Charleroi, Pennsylvania, had fronted the Ziegfeld Follies in 1915 and dozens of films, including *The Follies Girl* (1918) and *The Flapper* (1920). Rumors claimed suicide and murder, but Paris police ruled the death accidental. Roman Catholic cardinal Mundelein of Chicago was compelled to issue *The Danger of Hollywood: A Warning to Young Girls*—and who would know more about either Hollywood dangers or young girls than an aging priest? Thomas was twenty-five.

SEPTEMBER 12

2002—Nick Nolte's "Mug Shot"

One of the most famous arrest photos in history is no doubt a Polaroid snap of Nick Nolte by the Malibu Police Department, circulated on this date after the actor was arrested the previous day for suspicion of driving under the influence of drugs or alcohol. Nolte was pulled over by the California Highway Patrol when officers noticed the actor's black 1992 Mercedes-Benz swerving across a Malibu highway. A previous felony offender who had served five years' probation for selling fake draft cards in 1962, Omaha native Nolte pleaded no contest to the DUI charge and was given three years' probation with counseling with random testing. But the photo remains a bona fide classic, circulated worldwide, showing the star of the *48HRS* franchise, *The Prince of Tides* (1991), *Warrior* (2011) and other films scowling above a flowery Hawaiian shirt while his longish, unkempt blond hair spreads kinked in all directions in a hyper-Medusa-like arrangement. It wasn't the real mug shot, by the way, just a photo a policeman took at the booking.

SEPTEMBER 13

1971—ITALIAN BEAUTY FLAMES OUT
Actress Pier Angeli was actress Marisa Pavan's twin sister, James Dean's girlfriend, Kirk Douglas's fiancée and eventually Vic Damone's wife. The Sardinian beauty, christened Anna Maria Pierangeli, was the most striking Italian import of the Hollywood era of Anna Magnani, Sophia Loren, Gina Lollobrigida and Silvana Mangano. Pier starred in *Teresa* (1951), *Flame and the Flesh* (1954), *Somebody Up There Likes Me* (1956) and *Sodom and Gomorrah* (1963). Stage mother Enrica Pierangeli engineered the union with crooner Damone. Cast by director Francis Ford Coppola in *The Godfather* (1972), Pier never made it to the set. Her lifeless body was found on September 10, 1971, in her West Los Angeles home. An accidental barbiturate overdose was the official cause of death. She had divorced composer Armando Trovaioli in 1969 and supposedly never got over Dean's death. Her funeral service was held on this date at the Church of the Good Shepherd in Beverly Hills. She was thirty-nine.

SEPTEMBER 14

1982—PRINCESS GRACE: BING! BANG! BOOM!

Of all the female megastars who conquered the galaxy with make-them-stupid charm waves—Ingrid Bergman, Liz Taylor, Ava Gardner, Marilyn Monroe—none mowed down so many as quickly as ice princess Grace Kelly. By her marriage at age twenty-six to Prince Rainier of Monaco, she had as many star lovers as films: Gary Cooper, William Holden, Bing Crosby, Ray Milland, David Niven, Marlon Brando, Clark Gable, Tony Curtis, Cary Grant and Jean-Pierre Aumont. Another dozen included producer Anthony Havelock-Allan and designer Oleg Cassini. Brando and Bing engaged in fisticuffs after the latter caught Marlon and Grace *in flagrante delicto*. She maintained a French love nest for Frank Sinatra after her marriage. Her mother, with the byline Mrs. John B. Kelly, revealed much in a ten-part 1956 series, "My Daughter Grace Kelly: Her Life and Romances," in the *Los Angeles Herald-Examiner*. With mom naming names, Judy Garland's opinion on whether or not Grace was a nymphomaniac—"If she calmed down"—seems quaint. Grace suffered a stroke while driving in Monaco on September 13, 1982, and her car crashed down a mountainside. She died on this date of her injuries. She was fifty-two.

Grace Kelly is pictured between Wendell Corey (left) and James Stewart in Alfred Hitchcock's *Rear Window* (1954).

SEPTEMBER 15

1954—MARILYN CATCHES THE BREEZE

The famous image of Marilyn Monroe laughing joyously as her skirt is blown up above her waist by the blast from a subway vent was shot in New York for writer-director Billy Wilder's *The Seven Year Itch*. Standing atop a grate as a subway passes beneath, Marilyn enjoys the moment, exclaiming, "Oh, can you feel the breeze from the subway!? Isn't it delicious!?" An estimated five thousand spectators, mostly men, were drawn to Lexington Avenue and 52nd Street at 1:00 a.m. on this date by publicists and word of mouth to witness cinematographer Milton R. Krasner's many takes of the scene. While Marilyn seemed to enjoy showing off her panties, her husband, former New York Yankees center fielder and Big Apple icon Joe DiMaggio, cringed at her lighthearted exhibitionism, incidents replicated by the film *Insignificance* (1985).

SEPTEMBER 16

1974—DAVID CARRADINE'S FROLIC

Having ingested peyote, David Carradine wandered nude around his Laurel Canyon neighborhood on this date. With the drug in his head and the wind in his "boys," the star of TV's popular *Kung Fu* broke a window into a neighbor's home and bled onto the piano. He encountered a woman on the ramble and inquired if she was a witch. Police followed the blood trail back to his home. Carradine pleaded no contest to malicious mischief and was given probation. The young woman sued him for $1.1 million and was awarded $20,000. Actor John Carradine's son and elder bro to Keith and Robert Carradine, David had priors: disturbing the peace in San Francisco, shoplifting while in the army and marijuana possession in 1967. Afterward, he copped to pot possession in 1980 in South Africa and DUIs in 1984 and 1989. David's adventures ended in Bangkok, Thailand. His lifeless body was found hanging by a rope in a hotel closet on June 3, 2009, a victim of autoerotic asphyxiation. He was seventy-two.

SEPTEMBER 17

2008—RYAN O'NEAL: A MODEL FATHER

Actor Ryan O'Neal, who rocketed to fame in *Love Story* (1970) and later starred in such films as *Paper Moon* (1973), *Barry Lyndon* (1975) and *A Bridge Too Far* (1977), was arrested in his own home on this date along with his son, Redmond O'Neal. A probation officer, checking up on Redmond, discovered methamphetamine in the father's bedroom. On probation for two prior drug convictions, Redmond was held along with his father on $10,000 bail. Later, the elder O'Neal was ordered to participate in a drug awareness program. Redmond, the son of Farrah Fawcett, is the half brother of Tatum O'Neal and Griffin O'Neal (from Ryan's marriage with actress Joanna Cook Moore) and Patrick O'Neal (from Ryan's union with actress Leigh Taylor-Young). He was ordered to receive drug rehab on an outpatient basis.

SEPTEMBER 18

1932—HOLLYWOODLAND SWAN DIVE

A woman hiking beneath the Hollywoodland sign on this date found a woman's corpse. She bundled some remains—jacket, shoes and purse—and put them on the police station steps. Police speculated that the deceased had climbed a workman's ladder at the "H" and performed a swan dive. The LA County coroner said "multiple fractures of the pelvis" caused the death. Actress Peg Entwistle's body went unidentified until her suicide note was published in the newspapers. "I am afraid, I am a coward," the note read. "I am sorry for everything. If I had done this a long time ago, it would have saved a lot of pain. P.E." Peg married actor Robert Keith in 1927 and divorced him because he never told her about his son from a previous marriage, Brian Keith, the notable TV and film star who also committed suicide. The former Millicent Lilian Entwistle's only film was David O. Selznick's long delayed *Thirteen Women* (1935). Peg's burial site in Glendale, Ohio, was unmarked until a 2010 Facebook campaign led to its designation.

SEPTEMBER 19

1985—Out of the Closet and Into the Casket

A popular leading man opposite Doris Day, Liz Taylor, Jennifer Jones and others, Rock Hudson stolidly lived up to his name onscreen. At six feet, four inches, he was a strapping presence as well as a strong actor, especially as the Texas rancher in director George Stevens's *Giant* (1956). On July 25, 1985, America at large discovered that the former Roy Harold Scherer Jr. of Winnetka, Illinois, was suffering from acquired immune deficiency syndrome, or AIDS. Taylor urged her *Giant* costar to attend the AIDS Project Los Angeles's fundraiser on this date, but Hudson sent a prepared statement read by Burt Lancaster. It said that Rock realized his situation "brought enormous international attention to the gravity of this disease...and is leading to more research, more contribution of funds, and a better understanding of this disease than ever before." Less than a month later, Rock was dead from AIDS. He was fifty-nine.

Rock Hudson and Elizabeth Taylor costarred with Mercedes McCambridge (far right) in *Giant* (1956).

SEPTEMBER 20

1988—ACCIDENT CLAIMS KINNEAR

While on location filming director Richard Lester's *The Return of the Musketeers* (1989), British comic performer Roy Kinnear became one of the few actors to die after injuries sustained in an on-set accident. He fell from a horse during filming at Toledo, Spain, and broke his pelvis on September 19, 1988, and then died of a heart attack on this date at Ruber International Hospital in Madrid. He played Planchet, the servant of d'Artagnan. Roy created the character in Lester's *The Three Musketeers* (1973). Round-faced and heavy-set, Kinnear often played characters lampooning officialdom. His films include *How I Won the War* (1968), the original *Willy Wonka and the Chocolate Factory* (1971), Francis Ford Coppola's *Hammett* (1982) and multiple films for directors Sidney Lumet and Mel Brooks. He was fifty-four.

SEPTEMBER 21

1978—FALL GUY FOR FALL GUY A FALL GUY

A.J. Bakunas was considered one of the best stunt men in the business when one-upmanship led to his death. He doubled for George Kennedy in the film *Steel* (1979), starring Lee Majors, who had been TV's *The Six Million Dollar Man* and *The Fall Guy*. Bakunas previously had set a world record with a 230-foot fall in *Hooper* (1978), about stunt men. A.J.'s record was broken by Dar Robinson, who plummeted 286 feet for a non-movie stunt at Knotts Berry Farm in Buena Park, California. To take back fall-guy supremacy, Bakunas, who had already successfully jumped from nine stories up in Kincaid Towers in Lexington, Kentucky, for the *Steel* cameras, convinced Majors and director Steve Carver to let him do it again—this time from the twenty-second story or 315 feet. As one thousand people watched, A.J. was flawless once more. The equipment wasn't. The airbag designed to break his fall split on impact. Bakunas died of lung injuries the next day at University of Kentucky Good Samaritan Hospital. He was thirty.

SEPTEMBER 22

1995—*SHOWGIRLS*: SIZZLE, FIZZLE AND VIDEO

A melodramatic catfight with various sexual couplings set against a Vegas showbiz background, *Showgirls* was the first NC-17-rated film to receive a wide theatrical release, on this date. With leaden dialogue and gratuitous nudity, it was a triumph of screenwriter Joe Eszterhas's gall and director Paul Verhoeven's moxie in convincing MGM to heave $45 million at the project. Elizabeth Berkley plays a drifter-cum-stripper who becomes the lead performer of a topless casino extravaganza after she shoves her competition (Gina Gershon) into an injury. Kyle MacLachlan, Robert Davi and Glenn Plummer costarred. Devoid of redemption in Sin City, *Showgirls* features lap dances, stripping, prostitution, gross envy and humiliation. Critics hated it, audiences avoided it, but the picture became an all-time teen-sneak-in challenge at the multiplex. A box-office bomb, the film became one of MGM's top twenty earning productions in video release, making more than $100 million in the home-viewing market.

SEPTEMBER 23

1999—VAN DAMME'S AMERICAN DREAM

The Belgian-born kickboxing champ Jean-Claude Van Damme learned English, he said, by watching *The Flintstones*. His first jobs in America were waiter, taxi driver and bouncer at Woody's, Chuck Norris's Newport Beach, California nightclub. Van Damme eventually fulfilled his own notion of himself as the "Fred Astaire of karate" and starred in *Cyborg* (1989), *Universal Soldier* (1992), *Timecop* (1994) and others. After the fad of his fame faded, he found he couldn't muscle out of a DUI arrest on this date in Beverly Hills. He pleaded no contest, and on July 10, 2000, Van Damme was sentenced to an anti–drunk driving class, $1,200 in fines, three years' probation and a three-month revocation of his driving license. He turned down a role in Sly Stallone's lucrative geezer-fest *The Expendables* (2010) but saw the error of his ways and performed in Sly's *Expendables 2* (2012).

SEPTEMBER 24

2009—RANDY AND THE "STAR WHACKERS"

Randy Quaid and his wife, Evi, were granted asylum in Canada in October 2010. They told authorities that they feared for their lives in the States, claiming actors have died as victims of a cabal Quaid labeled the "Hollywood Star Whackers." On July 15, 2011, the U.S. Justice Department declined Santa Barbara County district attorney Joyce Dudley's attempt to extradite the Quaids to face felony burglary charges filed in September 2010. Randy and Evi were found illegally living in the guest house of their former residence, which they sold in 2007. They also skipped out on a $10,000 San Ysidro Ranch hotel bill but were nabbed in Presidio County, Texas. The hotel bill was paid, and charges were dropped against Dennis Quaid's brother, whose big mug was ubiquitous in *The Last Detail* (1973), *Independence Day* (1996), *Kingpin* (1996), *Brokeback Mountain* (2005) and others. The "Star Whackers" remain at large.

SEPTEMBER 25

1936—BUSBY BERKELEY'S TRIALS

The master of dance staging left a party at Warner Bros. producer William Koenig's home and was behind the wheel of his roadster on September 8, 1935, when the car crossed over into oncoming traffic on Roosevelt Highway and struck two other cars. Two people were killed instantly. One of five seriously injured others would also die from wounds incurred in the accident. Berkeley faced the shock of two counts of second-degree murder and not the expected manslaughter charges. He hired lawyer-to-the-stars Jerry Geisler. After two hung juries in the case, on Christmas Eve 1935 and April 17, 1936, a third trial jury acquitted Berkeley after deliberating an hour and a half. Berkeley's films after the trials included many as choreographer and a few as director, including *Babes in Arms* (1939) and other Mickey Rooney vehicles and *Take Me Out to the Ball Game* (1949).

Busby Berkeley, here with Mickey Rooney and Judy Garland, escaped murder charges after three sensational trials.

SEPTEMBER 26

1996—PAM AND TOMMY'S SOAP OPERA

Playboy model Pam Anderson's movie-star heyday came after *Baywatch* became a TV hit. Pam starred in *Snapdragon* (1993), *Raw Justice* (1994), *Baywatch the Movie: Forbidden Paradise* (1995) and *Barb Wire* (1996). Another item, *Pam & Tommy Lee: Stolen Honeymoon* (1996), her sex tape with rocker hubby Lee of Motley Crue, hit the video market, and the couple began making the police blotter. On this date at the Viper Room, Tommy Lee knocked over a photographer; he was convicted of battery, fined and sentenced to two years' probation and two hundred hours of community service. Pam filed for divorce two months later. In 1998, Tommy served six months in jail for spousal abuse after kicking Pam in their Malibu home. In 2007, he was ejected from the MTV Video Music Awards for starting a fight with Kid Rock, whom Pam married after her divorce from Tommy. Pam and Tommy have reunited and split several times since.

SEPTEMBER 27

1971—BLOOD AND GUTS: MAILER VERSUS TORN

The Norman Mailer–directed film *Maidstone* was released this week in New York. Shot in 1968, it concerns a movie director running for president. The film is infamous for an on-set fracas between Mailer, playing the lead, and the feisty Rip Torn as the director's brother. Torn struck Mailer in the head with a hammer during a knockdown, drag-out mêlée. The distinguished author of *The Naked and the Dead* (1948), *The Deer Park* (1955) and *An American Dream* (1965), Mailer—with cinematographer D.A. Pennebaker's camera rolling—grappled with Torn and bit him on the ear. Torn strangled Mailer, who rolled on top of the actor. The bloody tussle, broken up after the off-camera screaming started, is in the finished film as both actors bellow obscenities using their actual names. Generations later, *New York Times* critic A.O. Scott wrote that the film "captures something essential in Mr. Mailer—his reckless bravado, his willingness to court ridiculousness and the loss of control."

SEPTEMBER 28

1952—THE TONE WAS ALL WRONG

Franchot Tone, who received an Oscar nomination for *Mutiny on the Bounty* (1935), married Barbara Payton, a platinum-blonde starlet in *Bride of the Gorilla* (1951), on this date in Cloquet, Minnesota. Two weeks earlier, Tone had suffered a brain concussion and broken nose and cheekbone tangling with former Harvard boxer Tom Neal, star of *Detour* (1945) and *The Brute Man* (1946). The fight was over the charms of the already twice-divorced Miss Payton. "Tom Neal Knocks Out Tone in Love Fist Fight; Barbara Payton Hysterical After Brawl on Lawn," declared the front page of the *Los Angeles Herald and Express*. After fifty-three days with Tone, Babs went back to Neal for four years. Tone was granted a divorce the following May after he produced compromising photos of Payton and Neal. Babs drifted into prostitution and the bottle, pimping her lurid adventures for $1,000 in the ghost-written *I Am Not Ashamed* (1963). Ravaged by booze, she died on the floor of her parents' San Diego bathroom on May 8, 1967. She was thirty-nine.

SEPTEMBER 29

1953—Raft Springs Scarface's Bro

The LAPD invaded the room of John Capone in the Beverly Hills Hotel on this night, arresting the brother of the late Chicago mobster Al "Scarface" Capone and a pal, Joe Laino. As cynically reported by the *Los Angeles Times*, it was a roundup of the usual suspects. The charge was "suspicion of robbery, the customary 'roust' booking," claimed the *Times*. Also in the room was George Raft, a mob fringe dweller way before he costarred in Howard Hawks's *Scarface: The Shame of a Nation* (1932), famously flipping a coin in his scenes. Raft's friendships with racketeers included one with New York mobster Owney "The Killer" Madden. Raft used his influence, according to the *Times*, to spring Capone and Laino. Chided for misplaced loyalty and lavish spending late in life, Raft said, "Part of [my] ten million I spent on gambling, part on booze, part on women. The rest I spent foolishly."

SEPTEMBER 30

1955—JAMES DEAN AT FATEFUL CROSSROADS

The location was the meeting of California Highways 41 and 46, a mile east of Cholame, California. Protean Method actor and fast-rising star James Dean, front man of *Rebel Without a Cause* (1955), *East of Eden* (1955) and, posthumously, *Giant* (1956), was behind the wheel of his Porsche 550 Spyder. He was driving west on Highway 46 (then numbered 466) and reached the intersection of Highway 41. A Cal Poly student named Donald Turnupseed was turning onto 41 and entered

Dean's lane without apparently seeing him. Although evidence of the wreckage shows that Dean was probably only going fifty-five miles per hour, he was unable to stop. And so the most infamous automobile accident in the Hollywood galaxy took Dean in the prime of his much-heralded youth. Jimmy was twenty-four.

OCTOBER 1

1968—*NIGHT OF THE LIVING DEAD* A SHOCKER

The Fulton Theater in Pittsburgh was the staging venue on this date for the unexpected rise of the modern horror film, the "splatter-film" subgenre of gory, messy, in-your-face mayhem staged as if it could occur up your street. Gore special effects had been around before *Night of the Living Dead* premiered on this date but were used sparingly, for shock effect. Horror pictures also weren't so down-home, often using castles, other time periods and otherworldly ghouls. But director George A. Romero's shoestring-budget picture, about flesh-craving zombies run amok, poured on shock after cannibalistic shock. Reaction included critical revulsion. Shot in Pittsburgh, the film used unknown actors and everyday locales—but had a monstrous effect on the movie business. Such watershed franchise launchers as Tobe Hooper's *The Texas Chainsaw Massacre* (1974), John Carpenter's *Halloween* (1978), Sean S. Cunningham's *Friday the 13th* (1980) and Wes Craven's *A Nightmare on Elm Street* (1984) owe a debt of gratitude to Romero's gory, grainy, tacky, frightening and lucrative vision.

OCTOBER 2

Sean Penn was eventually sentenced to three years' probation and three hundred hours of community service for battery and vandalism against photographer Jordan Dawes for an incident on this date in Brentwood, California. Dawes was filming a story about paparazzi when Penn, who won Academy Awards for *Mystic River* (2003) and *Milk* (2008), began kicking and punching him. Dawes required knee surgery as a result of the attack. According to Dawes's civil suit, Penn had threatened to kill him, saying, "The next time I see you, you will be in a box." Penn's lawyer said, "Prolonging this matter in the court system would not have been in Mr. Penn's best interests and would have distracted from his charitable commitments, specifically his work in Haiti." Penn's efforts to help the victims of the 2010 Haiti earthquake led to his appointment in January 2012 as ambassador-at-large for Haiti.

OCTOBER 3

1995—O.J. SIMPSON—"NOT GUILTY"

One of the most famous verdicts in American jurisprudence was handed down in California Superior Court in Los Angeles on this date: Orenthal James Simpson walked away a free man, acquitted of murdering his wife and her boyfriend. In a subsequent civil suit charging O.J. with wrongful death, the jury awarded Brown and Simpson's children, Sydney and Justin, $12.6 million from their father as recipients of their mother's estate. The victims' families were awarded $33.5 million in compensatory and punitive damages. In the aftermath, tabloid witnesses, book deals and those claiming O.J. confessed to them came out of the woodwork. The Heisman Trophy winner and Pro Football Hall of Famer, sportscaster and movie actor, shambled off a broken man without a nickel. For a 2007 armed robbery of a sports memorabilia merchant in a Las Vegas hotel, "the Juice" received a thirty-three-year sentence from a Clark County, Nevada judge. O.J. sits in a Nevada prison.

OCTOBER 4

2004—*PAPER MOON* ACTRESS'S *PAPER LIFE*

A Paper Life, Tatum O'Neal's first autobiography, was released on this date by HarperCollins. Life in Hollywood was anything but a frolic in la-la land for the youngest performer to win a competitive Oscar. She was named best supporting actress for director Peter Bogdanovich's *Paper Moon* (1973), opposite her real-life father, Ryan O'Neal. Tatum wrote that her father beat her after she won her Oscar. Molested by her father's drug dealer, the star of *The Bad News Bears* (1976), *Little Darlings* (1980) and other movies became addicted to cocaine and heroin and attempted suicide. Melanie Griffith, Tatum avers, took her to her first orgy when the younger girl was twelve. Tatum's husband, tennis pro John McEnroe, beat her and treated her as if she was his slave. Because of her drug dependency, McEnroe was awarded custody of their three children. Ryan O'Neal refuted his daughter's claims in a prepared statement in 2008, the same year Tatum was busted for cocaine possession in New York. Her semi-corrective follow-up autobiography, *Found: A Daughter's Journey Home*, came out in 2011.

OCTOBER 5

1990—NC-17 RATING IS USED

Henry & June, director Philip Kaufman's film about the ménage à trois of Parisian writer Anais Nin and American novelist Henry Miller and his wife, was released on this date as the first film to receive the NC-17 rating from the Motion Picture Association of America. Prior to the use of NC-17, meaning no children under the age of seventeen would be admitted, several critically acclaimed films of strong adult subject matter had been stigmatized by the X rating or released without approval by the MPAA. They included, from the previous year, *Henry: Portrait of a Serial Killer* and *The Cook, the Thief, His Wife & Her Lover*. The X rating, which sends a message that a film is pornographic, had been attached to such films of merit as *Midnight Cowboy* (1969), *A Clockwork Orange* (1971), *Fritz the Cat* (1972) and *Last Tango in Paris* (1973). On September 27, the MPAA introduced the NC-17 rating as its official rating for adult-oriented films bearing the MPAA seal. *Henry & June* included love scenes between Anais (Maria de Medeiros) and June (Uma Thurman).

OCTOBER 6

Elizabeth Taylor went matrimonial for the eighth time, marrying her least famous catch, construction worker Larry Fortensky, at Michael Jackson's Neverland Ranch in Santa Barbara County, California. Her previous seven marriages were to a hotel tycoon, producer, politician, singer and a couple of British actors (Michael Wilding and Dick Burton twice). So for a luxury lover like Lizzie, Larry was a stray. The couple met in the Betty Ford dry-out tank, which isn't exactly a recipe for success. The "Fortenskys" divorced in 1996 because he was tired of being "Mr. Elizabeth Taylor." Since then, Larry has been arrested at least twice on drug charges. The construction worker fell down a San Juan Capistrano staircase in 1999 and was in a coma for six weeks. He snapped out of it and eventually got $800,000 in Liz's will.

OCTOBER 7

2003—"GOVERNATOR" ARNOLD ELECTED

Arnold Schwarzenegger, the world champion bodybuilder and international movie action star, sent a first-round series of shock waves through the political community when he sought a higher calling than dispatching bad guys with bad quips ("He always was a hothead," etc.). He was first elected governor of California on this date in a special recall race to replace then-governor Gray Davis. Arnold was sworn in on November 17, 2003, to serve the remainder of Davis's term and then was reelected on November 7, 2006, in California's gubernatorial election to serve a full term. Arnie followed such previous film stars into politics as Helen Gahagan Douglas, George Murphy, Ronald Reagan, Glenda Jackson, Clint Eastwood, et al. Arnold disappeared after a time into lame-duck land in Sacramento.

OCTOBER 8

RKO Radio Pictures released in Hollywood on this date *I Married a Communist!*, a hysterical picture about past Communist ties coming back to haunt an innocent man. Laraine Day and Robert Ryan starred in this strident effort by producer Howard Hughes to cash in on anti-Commie hysteria. Hughes also used the project to test the patriotism of his directors. Thirteen directors turned the project down, beginning with the eventually blacklisted Joseph Losey. *I Married a Communist!* was directed by British veteran Robert Stevenson, who later directed many Disney pictures, including the big hits *Old Yeller* (1957) and *Mary Poppins* (1964). Hughes later rereleased his Reds-reviling melodrama as *The Woman on Pier 13*.

OCTOBER 9

1951—A DAY IN THE LIFE OF LAWRENCE TIERNEY

The headline in the *New York Times* about Lawrence Tierney on this date proclaimed, "Actor Held After Affray." Previous headlines about the bartender, steelworker and actor were collected by the *Los Angeles Times* in Tierney's February 28, 2002 obit: "Film 'Dillinger' Booked on Drunk Charge," "Court Warns Film Actor to Be Good," "Actor Tierney Must Sleep on Jail Floor" and "Tierney Goes to Jail Again." The roughhouse, B-picture actor, the older brother of actor Scott Brady (Brady was born Gerald Tierney), had the requisites to add verisimilitude to *San Quentin* (1946), *Born to Kill* (1947), *The Hoodlum* (1951), *Kill or Be Killed* (1952) and *Reservoir Dogs* (1991). By 1958, Tierney had been arrested in either California or New York eleven times, mostly for brawling and drunkenness. He was stabbed in 1973 outside a New York bar. In 1975, a New York woman leaped to her death from a fourth-story window when he dropped by to say hello. "She just went out the window," he told police.

OCTOBER 10

2004—Reeve's Final Curtain

The movies' most prominent portrayer of Superman passed away after physical tribulations that might have demoralized a less resilient person. Christopher Reeve, who played the comic book hero beginning with *Superman* (1978), also contributed strong roles in *Deathtrap* (1982), *The Remains of the Day* (1993) and *Speechless* (1994). On May 27, 1995, the rangy Reeve, one of the American cinema's great figures of virility, was paralyzed from the neck down in a polo accident near Charlottesville, Virginia. At the Academy Awards ceremony in 1996, he appeared in a wheelchair to announce a montage of film clips regarding social issues and was given a two-minute ovation. An antibiotic for a pressure wound causing sepsis led to cardiac arrest and then a coma. He died on this date at Northern Westchester Hospital in Mount Kisco, New York. He was fifty-two.

OCTOBER 11

A report in the *Los Angeles Times* on this date gave an update on Jan-Michael Vincent, the star of the CBS-TV helicopter series *Airwolf* and one of the more promising stars of the 1970s. His latest role was mopping up in the Culver City jail, emptying garbage cans and delivering meals to inmates. Vincent costarred in films fronted by John Wayne, Charles Bronson and Gene Hackman and had twice played Robert Mitchum's son, in *Going Home* (1971) and the miniseries *The Winds of War* (1983). He was in demand on network TV when drugs and alcohol overtook him. His chores for the Culver City Police Department were part of a deal to work off time for parole violations. His transgressions included public drunkenness and assault. Vincent had broken his neck in a 1996 car crash. His last credit is *Escape to Grizzly Mountain* (2004). If Vincent, who was born on July 15, 1944, is alive as this book goes to print, he's sixty-eight.

OCTOBER 12

1984—Shooting a Bad Blank

Actor and model Jon-Erik Hexum, whose credits included the TV series *Voyagers!*, TV movie *Making of a Male Model* (1983) and the feature *The Bear* (1984), was declared brain-dead on October 18, 1984, and taken off life-support systems. The cause of death was wounds he received on this date on the set of his CBS-TV show, *Cover Up*, when, clowning around without any idea of the danger, he placed a .44 Magnum pistol loaded with blanks to his temple and pulled the trigger. His demise by his own doing was not a suicide but a freak work-related accident. The inexperienced Hexum did not know that blanks use paper wadding to keep the bullets' gunpowder in their shells. When Hexum pulled the trigger, the wadding was propelled with such force that it broke a piece of his skull, causing a massive brain hemorrhage. The New Jersey–born Hexum was cremated, and his ashes were scattered by his mother. He was twenty-six.

OCTOBER 13

The body of cowboy star Tom Mix was in Burbank, California, on this date, flown from Arizona after he was killed in a freak auto accident. The star of nearly four hundred films since 1909, mostly westerns, Mix had been traveling on October 12, 1940, at speeds near eighty miles per hour in his Cord auto on State Route 79 near Florence, Arizona. He hit the brakes for construction barriers at a drop-off where a bridge had been washed out by a flash flood. An aluminum suitcase containing money and jewels, which Mix had placed on a shelf behind him in the car, flew forward and struck the back of his head, shattering his skull and breaking his neck. The actor was in Arizona visiting an old friend, Pima County sheriff Ed Nichols, in Tucson. A work crew witnessed his car swerve and roll into a gully. A small museum at his birthplace, Mix Run, Pennsylvania, commemorates his life, and a stone monument erected at the crash site in Pinal County, Arizona, memorializes his death. Mix was sixty.

OCTOBER 14

Jeff Goldblum and Geena Davis were an offbeat couple, both tall, talented and good together in *Transylvania 6-5000* (1985), director David Cronenberg's remake of *The Fly* (1986) and *Earth Girls Are Easy* (1988)—even if the public stayed away from the first and third of these titles. The split on this date was due to the usual "irreconcilable differences." They both went on to bigger and better things, him to Steven Spielberg's *Jurassic Park* (1993) and *Independence Day* (1996). Davis had won the Oscar for best supporting actress for *The Accidental Tourist* (1987) and was nominated for best actress for *Thelma & Louise* (1991) and won Golden Globes for *A League of Their Own* (1992) and the TV series *Commander in Chief* (2005). An odd postscript occurred in 2001, when reports claimed Liz Taylor, sixty-nine, was dating Goldblum, then forty-eight.

OCTOBER 15

1969—No Fixing This Wagon

Investing $25 million in 1968 dollars in the singular anomaly of a Lee Marvin–Clint Eastwood *musical*, Metro-Goldwyn-Mayer released *Paint Your Wagon* in the United States on this date. One of the costliest flops of all time, the film about the California Gold Rush has nonetheless sustained a lively TV life. A job of ridiculous excess bobbled by director Joshua Logan—who had made *Bus Stop* (1956), *South Pacific* (1958) and other excellent films—the location shoot in the mountains of Oregon finished off his Hollywood career. It also sapped MGM's savings, sent the bibulous and roving Marvin on an on-set binge and ingrained in Eastwood a frugality that served him well later in his superlative producing and directing careers. One Logan quote defines the cohesiveness on the set: "Not since Attila the Hun swept across Europe leaving 500 years of total blackness, has there been a man like Lee Marvin."

OCTOBER 16

One of America's dynamic performers, the rangy, cannon-voiced Raul Julia, suffered a stroke on this date. After attending a play, he felt intense abdominal pain and was rushed by ambulance to North Shore University Hospital in Manhasset, Long Island, New York. This was within a year of a stomach operation and a bout of severe food poisoning on location for director John Frankenheimer's *The Burning Season* (1994) in Chiapas, Mexico. The stroke hit in the hospital. Julia fell into a coma on October 20 and was put on life support. Four days later, on October 24, 1994, he died of a brain hemorrhage. His legacy includes three Tony Award nominations and memorable work in *Kiss of the Spider Woman* (1985), *Romero* (1989), *The Addams Family* (1991) and other films. He was fifty-four.

OCTOBER 17

As an original *Ocean's Eleven* (1960) conspirator with Frank Sinatra, Dean Martin, et al., Joey Bishop played one of the ex-army buddies who knock over Las Vegas casinos (two generations before George Clooney, Matt Damon and the boys repackaged the plot for Steven Soderbergh's franchise). As such, Joey joined Sinatra's Rat Pack, that ad-hoc, tavern-slouching royalty. Trouble was, over time, Rat Pack status became the thing for which Joey was most noted. After the other principals faced their final curtains, Joey was often identified as the "last surviving member of the Rat Pack," which irritated him. The former Joseph Abraham Gottlieb of the Bronx, New York, had starred on game shows, his own sitcom, namesake talk show, as an alternative guest host on *The Tonight Show* and in such movies as *The Naked and the Dead* (1958), *Sergeants 3* (1962), *Valley of the Dolls* (1967) and others. When he kicked the bucket in Newport Beach on this date, he didn't have to hear "Rat Pack" anymore. He was eighty-nine.

OCTOBER 18

Hollywood's No. 1 power couple of the 1990s called it quits in the new century. Bruce Willis, star of the *Die Hard* franchise, *Pulp Fiction* (1994), *Armageddon* (1998) and dozens of other action pictures, on this date divorced Demi Moore, an original Brat Pack actress who starred in *Ghost* (1990), *A Few Good Men* (1992) and *Striptease* (1996), among others. They had three daughters—Rumer, Scout LaRue and Tallulah Belle—and spent much of their off-Hollywood time in Hailey, Idaho, where Willis still owns businesses. No public reason was given for the breakup, but Bruce did say, "I felt I had failed as a father and a husband by not being able to make it work." Moore married the actor Ashton Kutcher, who replaced Charlie Sheen on the sitcom *Two and Half Men*. Willis attended their wedding. Demi later split with Kutcher and put in a rehab stint. Brucie married actress and model Emma Heming in 2009, and the couple had a daughter in 2012.

OCTOBER 19

1978—HIS FINAL GIG A TRAGIC ONE

Byron Elsworth Barr of St. Cloud, Minnesota, changed his name to Gig Young after his character in the Barbara Stanwyck vehicle *The Gay Sisters* (1942). He forged a career as the best friend or other guy in *Come Fill the Cup* (1951), *Young at Heart* (1954), *That Touch of Mink* (1962) and others. His engagement to Broadway actress Elaine Stritch was dropped so he could marry Elizabeth Montgomery in 1956, a union that was opposed by her father, actor-producer Robert Montgomery, and lasted to her 1963 sitcom stardom in *Bewitched*. Young won the best supporting actor Oscar as the marathon dance host in Sydney Pollack's *They Shoot Horses, Don't They?* (1969). Young's drinking increased with his marriages, the fifth one to Kim Schmidt. Three weeks after the nuptials, police found their bodies on this date in their Manhattan apartment and determined that he had shot her and then turned the gun on himself. Young left his Oscar to his agent, Marty Baum.

OCTOBER 20

1947—ANTI-RED HYSTERIA

The House Un-American Activities Committee's investigation into Hollywood's supposed Communist agenda during the post–World War II cold war began on this day, resulting in the blacklisting of uncooperative witnesses. Many who refused to testify as to the politics of their coworkers and friends were later jailed or just frozen out of the business. The most famous of these "unfriendly witnesses" were the "Hollywood Ten," mostly screenwriters: Herbert J. Biberman, Lester Cole, Edward Dmytryk, Ring Lardner Jr., John Howard Lawson, Albert Maltz, Samuel Ornitz, Adrian Scott, Dalton Trumbo and Alvah Bessie. A few writers found work under pseudonyms, especially in the burgeoning medium of television. But many of them suffered. Writer-director Billy Wilder, who poked fun at many institutions, including politics, proclaimed two of the "Hollywood Ten" talented, and "the rest were just unfriendly."

OCTOBER 21

Marie McDonald was found dead of a drug overdose on this date in Calabasas, California. Born Cora Marie Frye in Burgin, Kentucky, Marie was the "Body Beautiful" when she danced at the Florentine Gardens in Hollywood. The nickname was shortened to "The Body" when she became a magazine pin-up girl. Her seven marriages were interrupted by mistress duties for racketeer Bugsy Siegel. Her films include *The Geisha Boy* (1958) and *Promises! Promises!* (1963), and her marriages include two to shoe tycoon Harry Karl, who later married Debbie Reynolds. Marie dated Eddie Fisher and Michael Wilding, two of Liz Taylor's ex-hubbies, and suffered miscarriages before giving birth to a daughter. Marie's dates, auto accidents, psychiatric clinic escapades and contention in 1957 that she was kidnapped kept the tabloids busy. Her sixth husband, Donald F. Taylor, committed suicide three months after her death. Marie was forty-two.

OCTOBER 22

1993—IN LIKE FLINT IN TWILIGHT YEARS

James Coburn was sixty-five and actress Paula O'Hara Murad thirty-eight when they married on this date—another of those age-disparity unions that the tabloid press loves to watch. However, a measure of reinvigoration seemed to come to the lanky, silver-haired action star of such hits as *The Magnificent Seven* (1960), *The Great Escape* (1963), *Our Man Flint* (1965) and *Cross of Iron* (1977). He enjoyed a twilight run as a character player, including in *Eraser* (1996) and *Payback* (1999), and as a voice-over narrator, memorably for Chevy trucks ("Like a rock!"). He took home the Oscar for best supporting actor as Nick Nolte's miserly dad in director Paul Schrader's *Affliction* (1998). Paula was the second wife for the Laurel, Nebraska–born and Compton, California–raised Coburn. They remained together until his death from a heart attack on November 18, 2002. He was seventy-four. She died from cancer in 2004 at the age of forty-eight.

OCTOBER 23

1957—*AND GOD CREATED WOMAN*

Director Roger Vadim's original French film about a seductress romancing her way through the males on the beaches of St. Tropez opened in New York City during this week. As the most lucrative foreign film yet released in America, it supported the notion that the more discerning filmgoer didn't just prefer the artistic and intellectual merits of European movies; he or she also liked the imports because they were sexier. The picture introduced to American audiences the statuesque Brigitte Bardot, labeled a "cineminx" by *Time* magazine. The mere title plus the poster, associating the Lord with an image of Ms. Bardot, let alone the plot and her relative absence of a wardrobe, sent the National Legion of Decency into paroxysms. It huffed a firm condemnation, drawing more people to the picture out of curiosity. Generations later, after he directed his then-wife Jane Fonda in *Circle of Love* (1964) and *Barbarella* (1968), Vadim remade *And God Created Woman* (1988) with Rebecca De Mornay.

OCTOBER 24

1951—Shoeless Lawrence Tierney

Fads and trends come and go, even among the habitually intoxicated and incarcerated. Tough-guy actor Lawrence Tierney, who starred in *Dillinger* (1945), *The Devil Thumbs a Ride* (1947) and many other films noir, was arrested for the thirteenth time on this date. Getting more time in the bucket wasn't unusual for Tierney, but this was the second time in two weeks that he was arrested without his shoes. You might think that a guy popular in pictures could keep himself in Oxblood Cordovans with some Converse on the side. He walked shoeless into a Hollywood bar and offered to "Whip anybody in the house!" according to the Associated Press report. His previous arrest, number twelve, was two weeks earlier for causing a disturbance in a Santa Monica church. He was absent footwear on that occasion too (see October 9).

OCTOBER 25

1946—AVA BOUNCES HUBBY NO. 2

MGM contract beauty Ava Gardner got tired of hearing her second husband, clarinetist and bandleader Artie Shaw, tell her to improve her intellect. So she divorced Artie on this date, dissolving her second marriage after an earlier divorce from Mickey Rooney. She enjoyed her freedom until Frank Sinatra came sniffing around in the 1950s. As far as Frank was concerned, intellect had nothing to do with his ring-a-ding-ding magnetism to the sinuous and earthy Ava. He was so jealous that he followed her to African locations for John Ford's *Mogambo* (1953) with Clark Gable. As for Artie, he had a reputation for verbal abuse, to which some

of his eight wives have testified. Lana Turner suffered a nervous breakdown before she divorced him, but Evelyn Keyes stayed with him for twenty-eight years. Ava and Frank split eventually, and she virtually abandoned Hollywood after *Night of the Iguana* (1965), moving to Europe.

OCTOBER 26

2010—HIDE THE BREAKABLES: CHARLIE'S HERE!

Charlie Sheen lived up to his own billing as a "bitchin', a total freakin' rock star from Mars" on this date when, true to rock-star form, he trashed his room at the Plaza Hotel in New York. He reportedly cut down on his hookers this time—only one—which didn't keep him from ensconcing then-wife Denise Richards and his two kids, Lola and Sam, on the eighteenth floor while he flew higher on an upper level. Charlie damaged the chandelier and furniture in his room to the tune of $7,000. Denise eventually convinced him to check into New York–Presbyterian/Columbia University Medical Center. Sheen's representation blamed the room-trashing on a bad reaction to medication. Charlie and Denise divorced, and she took up with rocker Richie Sambora and then split with him over differences about Charlie. Sambora didn't like Charlie and Denise remaining in touch over issues dealing with their kids.

OCTOBER 27

In one of the wilder plots ever hatched, *Hustler* magazine publisher Larry Flynt supposedly hired a hit man in 1983 for $1 million to bump off Frank Sinatra, *Playboy* publisher Hugh Hefner, *Penthouse* publisher Bob Guccione and former *TV Guide* publisher Walter Annenberg. A Flynt associate intercepted the signed check as the proposed hit man was leaving Larry's office. Larry's lawyers subsequently denied the plot. This was no cooked-up hoax; it was related by Los Angeles County sheriff Sherman Block to KNBC-TV in Los Angeles on this date, five years after the fact. KNBC televised a photo of the check. The alleged hit man, Mitchell WerBell (aka WerBel), died in December 1983 at age sixty-five. A veteran OSS operative in World War II Indochina, WerBell was a mercenary trainer in Vietnam and Central America. He had been indicted several times for selling machine guns, and his last known residence was in Decatur, Georgia. As if this all didn't constitute enough urban legend, testimony in the *Cotton Club* murder trial held that WerBell was murdered, a victim of old-fashioned poisoning.

OCTOBER 28

1939—ALICE BRADY GONE, HER OSCAR, TOO

Alice Brady was one of Hollywood's most admired character actresses, a veteran of silent pictures since 1914 and an impressive presence in such films as *When Ladies Meet* (1933), *The Gay Divorcée* (1934) and her final movie, John Ford's *Young Mr. Lincoln* (1939). She was nominated for an Oscar for best supporting actress for *My Man Godfrey* (1936), and she won the statuette in the same category the following year in the reenactment of the Great Chicago Fire of 1871, *In Old Chicago* (1937). One of the ones taken before her time, Alice died from cancer on this date, five days before her forty-seventh birthday. During the Academy Awards presentation dinner the previous year, on March 10, 1938, at the Biltmore Hotel in Los Angeles, Brady's Oscar statuette was accepted by a man who supposedly was acting on the actress's behalf. The stolen Oscar was never recovered and the impostor never caught. The academy issued a replacement statuette, which was presented to Brady before her death.

OCTOBER 29

2004—KIEFER'S DRUNK DRIVING

Kiefer Sutherland's third DUI arrest occurred on this date. In 1989, the costar of *Stand by Me* (1986), *The Lost Boys* (1987), *Young Guns* (1988) and other movies was arrested for driving under the influence and carrying a concealed and loaded weapon. In a deal with prosecutors, the son of Canadian film star Donald Sutherland pleaded no contest to alcohol-related reckless driving. The other charges were dropped. Sutherland was arrested again for a DUI in 1993, pleaded no contest and performed 211 hours of community service. For this 2004 arrest, Sutherland was given five years' probation. Pushing his luck with Scotch doubles, the actor was arrested for a fourth DUI offense on September 25, 2007. This time he was released on $25,000 bail, pleaded no contest, had parole violation on top of everything else and surrendered to the Glendale, California police. The star of the long-running espionage series *24*, Sutherland served a forty-eight-day sentence in the Glendale City Jail, performing laundry and kitchen duties.

OCTOBER 30

1998—FARRAH-BASHING, FOR REAL

Writer-director James Orr began serving his three years' probation on this date for slamming Farrah Fawcett's head to the ground and choking and kicking her. One hundred hours of community service was tagged onto the sentence by Los Angeles County Superior Court judge Robert T. Altman, along with counseling and a $500 payment to a domestic violence fund. Orr was ordered to avoid any contact with Fawcett. The brawl occurred after the star of the original *Charlie's Angels* on ABC-TV and movies including *Extremities* (1986) took several swings at Orr's car with a baseball bat. Fawcett, whose less perilous romances were with actors Lee Majors and Ryan O'Neal, reportedly asked police to drop the charges against Orr, the screenwriter of *Three Men and a Baby* (1987) and *Mr. Destiny* (1990) and the writer-director of the film the two made together, *Man of the House* (1995). Orr was prosecuted and convicted anyway.

OCTOBER 31

1993—CRY ME A RIVER AT THE VIPER ROOM

One of the most promising young actors of his generation, River Phoenix had starred in such hit films as *Stand by Me* (1986), *Running on Empty* (1988), *Indiana Jones and the Last Crusade* (1989) and *My Own Private Idaho* (1991) by the time he celebrated this Halloween night in the Viper Room, the Sunset Strip nightclub owned by Johnny Depp. Phoenix was to perform that night with his friend Flea (Michael Balzary of the Red Hot Chili Peppers). The ugliness this night had nothing to do with costumes or masks—it coursed in River's veins. He collapsed on the sidewalk outside the club. His brother, Joaquin Phoenix, who would later garner an Oscar nomination for playing Johnny Cash in *Walk the Line* (2005), called 911. River was rushed to Cedars-Sinai Medical Center, where he was pronounced dead from an overdose of both heroin and cocaine, known as a "speedball." River was twenty-three.

NOVEMBER 1

2006—ADRIENNE SHELLY MURDERED

Adrienne Shelly had forged a unique career, particularly as a star of director Hal Hartley's films *The Unbelievable Truth* (1989) and *Trust* (1990), as well as in the wild trailer-trash epic *Hold Me! Thrill Me! Kiss Me!* (1992). She wrote and directed *Waitress* (2006), in which she costarred with Keri Russell and Andy Griffith. She also wrote *Serious Moonlight* (2009) starring Meg Ryan. Adrienne was found by her husband, producer Andrew Ostroy, on this date, hanging by a bedsheet from a shower rod in her Manhattan apartment. Police arrested a nineteen-year-old Ecuadoran national, Diego Pillco, who worked for a company renovating Shelly's building. Pillco confessed to encountering the victim during his robbery of her apartment. He struggled with her when she tried to call 911 and then hanged her to make the death appear like a suicide. Pillco was sentenced to twenty-five years in prison and then deportation. Adrienne was forty.

NOVEMBER 2

1990—CHEYENNE BRANDO'S SUICIDE TRIES

News reached American shores that Marlon Brando's daughter Cheyenne, twenty, lay comatose in a Tahitian hospital on this date after an overdose of tranquilizers and antidepressant drugs. Physicians at Mamao Hospital told the actor it was touch-and-go. The former model's half brother, Christian Brando, killed her lover, Dag Drollet, in May 1990 in Marlon's Mulholland Drive home, ostensibly to help extricate her from a bad relationship with Drollet. Christian eventually served six years on a manslaughter conviction after a media-blanketed courtroom circus that vacated the papers once the O.J. Simpson case became the cause célèbre. Cheyenne recovered from this suicidal episode only to attempt her own demise twice more. She succeeded on April 16, 1995, hanging herself in the seclusion of her Tahitian home. She was twenty-five.

NOVEMBER 3

1970—JANE FONDA ARRESTED IN CLEVELAND

Henry Fonda's daughter was arrested on suspicion of drug smuggling on this date at the Cleveland Airport as she was returning from an anti–Vietnam War rally in Canada. The cops confiscated her vitamins and photocopied her address book. The actress had just finished working on *Klute* (1971), in which she played a New York hooker, and for which she eventually won an Oscar, and her widely circulated mug shot shows her with a distinctly short haircut. At the time, the Nixon White House and J. Edgar Hoover's FBI considered Fonda a menace for inciting campus unrest around the country against the increasingly unpopular war. She was released on bond. Months later, after the analysis of her vitamins found no illicit narcotics, the charges were dropped. In 2012, Fonda allowed the charity known as the Georgia Campaign for Adolescent Pregnancy Prevention to raise money using her mug shot on T-shirts, mugs and tea towels.

NOVEMBER 4

1968—RAMON NOVARRO'S FUNERAL

One thousand people paid their respects on this date to one of MGM's prominent silent-era actors, Ramon Novarro, the star of *Ben-Hur: A Tale of the Christ* (1925), as well as *The Pagan* (1929), *In Gay Madrid* (1930) and others into the sound era. The Mexican-born Novarro, who constantly wrestled with his homosexuality in opposition to his Catholic upbringing, refused studio boss Louis B. Mayer's weighty suggestion that he go through with an arranged "lavender marriage." He remained a bachelor, hiring hustlers. On October 30, 1968, brothers Tom and Paul Ferguson arrived at his Studio City estate and, after drinks and sex, proceeded to try to rob Novarro, who kept little money on the premises. Paul Ferguson tied up the actor and beat him for several hours with a silver cane before the brothers left. Novarro choked to death on his own blood. Paul was sentenced in 1969 to life imprisonment for the murder but was paroled after seven years. Novarro was sixty-nine.

NOVEMBER 5

1960—WARD BOND KEELS OVER

The burly Ward Bond finally made top stardom on the most popular western television show in the heyday of TV westerns, the late 1950s. As Major Seth Adams, Bond led *Wagon Train* out of "St. Joe," Missouri, every September and arrived in California each spring. The wagon trains rolled annually from 1957 through 1965, but its first trail boss only made it to this date. He died of a heart attack in Dallas, Texas, and America mourned his unexpected passing. A former University of Southern California football player who had broken into films with fellow USC lineman Marion Morrison, later known as John Wayne, Bond costarred in seventeen of the Duke's pictures, many of them directed by John Ford. Bond's final feature was with Wayne in director Howard Hawks's *Rio Bravo* (1959). In his will, Bond left Wayne a shotgun with which the Duke once accidentally shot him. Bond was fifty-seven.

NOVEMBER 6

Universal Studios has had a long tradition of catching on fire (see June 3). A massive fire started deliberately on the back lot destroyed one-fifth of the standing sets on this date. The total damage was estimated at more than $25 million. The flames were started in a Brownstone Street alley by a security guard using a cigarette lighter, and high winds fanned their spread. One of Los Angeles's largest fires required four hundred firefighters from eighty-six companies employing six helicopters to get the blaze under control. Destroyed were New York Street, the *Ben-Hur* set and Courthouse Square, used by the *Back to the Future* franchise. More than twenty period autos used in the Sly Stallone film *Oscar* (1991) were destroyed. The disgruntled guard, Michael John Huston, pled guilty to arson. He had been employed by Burns International (not kidding) and was hired to watch over the cars. He was sentenced to four years in prison by Los Angeles Superior Court judge William R. Pounders in January 1992. Rebuilding began on November 26, 1990.

NOVEMBER 7

1951—FRANK DUMPS NANCY FOR AVA

Frank Sinatra, his career on the skids and the Catholics giving him grief, officially severed ties to his first wife, Nancy—the mother of his three children—in October 1951. With the ink still soggy on the divorce documents, he married Ava Gardner in Philadelphia on this date. The Catholic Church–based National Legion of Decency, with nothing better to do, had breathed down Frank's neck when the scandal sheets and society gossip mentioned his squiring of the sinuous Ava. The legion threatened a boycott of her films. Her reaction was amazement at the "prurient mass hysteria about a male and female climbing into bed and doing what comes naturally." The star of *One Touch of Venus* (1948), *Mogambo* (1953), *The Barefoot Contessa* (1954) and other hit films remained Mrs. Frank until 1957 and

was said to be the one woman Frank couldn't control. One of her wisecracks about the then-wispy Italian American saloon singer that has had a long life in underground culture was that Frank was "only 110 pounds, but 10 pounds of it is cock!"

Frank Sinatra costarred with Betty Garrett in *On the Town* (1949).

NOVEMBER 8

1951—Bob Mitchum Walks into a Bar...

Bernie Reynolds was one of the top five ranked heavyweights in the world and doing a hitch in the army in 1951 when he and Robert Mitchum made acquaintances, and then the papers, for one of the more notable unsanctioned bouts of the midcentury. Big Bad Bob, on location in Colorado Springs for Howard Hughes's Korean War picture *One Minute to Zero* (1952), was slaking his thirst with army extras in the Red Fox Bar of the Alamo Hotel when a

well-lubricated Reynolds swung at him and instead hit the wall. The actor clobbered him with a right, and it was lights out. It was a preamble to Bernie's last five contests after the army, including knockouts by Rocky Marciano and Ezzard Charles.

NOVEMBER 9

1936—JOHN BARRYMORE ELOPES

Actress Elaine Barrie, twenty-one, became the fourth Mrs. John Barrymore on this date. The fifty-five-year-old brother of Lionel and Ethel Barrymore and paternal grandfather of Drew Barrymore eloped with Barrie on this date to Mexico. Elaine acted in three films, one of those the short *How to Undress in Front of Your Husband* (1937). By the time of his marriage to Barrie, "Jack" was deep in his cups and debt, and the union only lasted until 1940. The general notion is that he wasted his magnificent talent, preferring to booze with cronies Errol Flynn, W.C. Fields, director Raoul Walsh and writer Gene Fowler. He died on May 29, 1942, at the age of sixty after collapsing on the air during Rudy Vallee's radio show. Walsh borrowed Barrymore's body from the funeral home and propped it up in Flynn's living room to give the surviving star a fright after a bibulous night. The gag was re-created in the film *W.C. Fields and Me* (1976).

NOVEMBER 10

2006—JACK PALANCE BOWS OUT

The most demonstrably virile Oscar winner of all time was depleted of all energy on this date. The former Volodymyr Palahniuk of Luzerne County, Pennsylvania, expired of natural causes at his daughter Holly's home in Montecito, California. Jack Palance, who forged a career as one of the movies' greatest villains in *Panic in the Streets* (1950), *Sudden Fear* (1952), *Shane* (1953) and other pictures, also made the grade as a rugged, imposing hero, including in the film for which he won the Oscar for best supporting actor, *City Slickers* (1991). Accepting the Oscar on March 30, 1992, the rangy seventy-three-year-old performed one-handed pushups on the stage after a verbal potshot at host Billy Crystal, who, coincidentally, was his costar in *City Slickers*: "Billy Crystal…hah!…I crap bigger than him." Crystal peppered the rest of the telecast with jabs at Jack's prowess: that Palance just "bungee-jumped from the Hollywood sign"…fathered all the children in a production number…had been named *People*'s "Sexiest Man Alive," etc. Jack was eighty-seven.

NOVEMBER 11

2005—KEITH ANDES CALLS IT QUITS

Keith Andes's dimensions and blond good looks made him, briefly, a leading man in Hollywood and on Broadway. He played Marilyn Monroe's boyfriend in the film version of Clifford Odets's *Clash by Night* (1952) and starred opposite Lucille Ball on Broadway in *Wildcat* (1960). A native of Ocean City, New Jersey, the six-foot, four-inch John Charles Andes graduated from Temple University and joined the U.S. Air Force before gaining a role in Moss Hart's play, *Winged Victory*, and the 1944 film made from it. Andes became familiar on dozens of TV shows, and his films include *Back from Eternity* (1956), *Tora! Tora! Tora!* (1970) and *...And Justice for All* (1979). Twice married, he had two sons. But upon learning that bladder cancer was advancing, he ended it all on this date in Canyon Country, Santa Clarita, California. The Los Angeles County coroner ruled the death a suicide by asphyxiation. Keith was eighty-five.

NOVEMBER 12

2003—Teen Star's Tepid Adulthood

In another case of early adulthood and declining acting career equaling despairing funk, Jonathan Brandis hanged himself on this date in his apartment on Detroit Avenue in Los Angeles. He died from injuries sustained in the hanging after being rushed to Cedars-Sinai Medical Center. A costar of such films as *Stepfather II* (1989) and *Sidekicks* (1992), as well as the series *seaQuest DSV* and the miniseries adaptation of Stephen King's *It* (1990), Brandis was upset when he was informed that his supporting role in the Bruce Willis film *Hart's War* (2002) had been cut from the final print. Brandis had anticipated the picture as his comeback vehicle. During his successful years, Brandis was a favorite of teen magazines and had dated *Fresh Prince of Bel-Air* star Tatyana Ali for nearly six years. The Danbury, Connecticut native was twenty-seven.

NOVEMBER 13

1960—BLACK AND WHITE IN COLOR

Like many a red-blooded American male, Sammy Davis Jr.
liked blondes. His covert relationship with blonde bombshell
Kim Novak, the star of *Pal Joey* (1957) with Frank Sinatra
and Alfred Hitchcock's *Vertigo* (1958) and other films, never
leaked details until Wil Haygood wrote about it in *In Black
and White: The Life of Sammy Davis Jr.* (2003). But interracial
relationships were taboo in American society, and interracial
marriage was a crime in thirty-one states. On this date,
Sammy married May Britt, the Swedish-born star of such
films as *The Young Lions* (1958) and the remake of *The Blue
Angel* (1959). As the rumor went, the Kennedys told Sinatra
to have then-Democratic supporter Sammy hold off on the
nuptials until after the 1960 presidential election earlier
that month. The crime of interracial marriage was still on
the books in seventeen states in 1967, when it was ruled
unconstitutional by the U.S. Supreme Court. The Davises
divorced in 1968 when May learned of one of Sammy's
affairs, with actress-dancer Lola Falana.

NOVEMBER 14

1964—*SANTA CLAUS CONQUERS THE MARTIANS*

One of the worst movies ever made, released on this date, combined sci-fi idiocy with yuletide timing. The Martians, having no one to give their progeny presents, kidnap Kris Kringle. You couldn't make that up with a straight face on a bar napkin at 2:00 a.m.—these days or even then. But producer Paul L. Jacobson devised the story, Glenville Mareth fleshed out a script and TV series veteran Nicholas Webster directed it with what appears to have been a grocery-list budget. John Call, a TV vet, played Santa. The only other recognizable cast members were future nude model and bimbo-starlet Pia Zadora, then a ten-year-old moppet, and Bill McCutcheon, who won a 1988 Tony Award for best performance in a featured role for *Anything Goes*. Often ranked among the worst movies ever made, *Santa Claus Conquers the Martians* is on the Bottom 100 list of worst pictures compiled by the Internet Movie Database.

NOVEMBER 15

1958—TY POWER: AN EARLY EXIT

Tyrone Power was one of Twentieth Century-Fox's biggest stars, a bankable, reliable presence in costumers requiring swordplay but solid in every genre: *In Old Chicago* (1937), *Jesse James* (1939), *The Mark of Zorro* (1940), *Blood and Sand* (1941), etc. Henry King, who directed Power in eleven pictures, introduced him to flying, and it  became a big part of his life. In World War II as a marine corps pilot, Ty flew cargo and munitions into the Battles of Iwo Jima and Okinawa and flew out wounded marines. It was a shock to many on this date when he suffered a fatal heart attack on location in Madrid, Spain, amid filming a fencing duel with George Sanders for director King Vidor's epic *Solomon and Sheba* (1959). Ty died moments after being put into an ambulance. He was replaced by Yul Brynner, but some of his swordplay scenes can be detected in the final cut. A son of Cincinnati, Ohio, Power was buried in Hollywood. At the graveside service, Laurence Olivier recited the poem "High Flight." Power was forty-four.

NOVEMBER 16

1981—WILLIAM HOLDEN: DEAD DRUNK

The body of the star of *Sunset Boulevard* (1950), *Stalag 17* (1953), *Picnic* (1955), *The Bridge on the River Kwai* (1957), *The Wild Bunch* (1969), *Network* (1977) and other classics was found decomposed on this date in a Santa Monica hotel room. A lifelong boozer, Holden, alone, fell and hit his head on a table and bled to death. Possessed of superb talent and insane handsomeness—a top box-office draw—Holden was judged by some, including the great filmmaker Billy Wilder, to be the perfect movie star. He so thoroughly represented the American male of the postwar age, bringing intelligence, resolve, inherent cynicism and doubt,

worldliness and depth of feeling to each role he played. Holden had been married three times and was best man at Ronald Reagan's second wedding. His ashes were scattered in the Pacific Ocean. He was sixty-three.

William Holden (left) and Sir Alec Guinness starred in Sir David Lean's *The Bridge on the River Kwai* (1957).

NOVEMBER 17

A favorite star of pioneering writer-director Lois Weber's silent-era movies, Universal Pictures contract star Marie Walcamp was often presented as an action heroine in the mold of Ruth Roland and Pearl White in westerns and serials. The blonde Dennison, Ohio native played a Native American in *The Werewolf* (1913) at age nineteen, and her films include *Liberty, a Daughter of the U.S.A.* (1916), a western serial in which she costarred as a young heiress with Jack Holt, and Weber's socially conscious films: *Hop—The Devil's Brew* (1916), the anti-abortion melodrama *Where Are My Children?* (1916) and *The Blot* (1921). Out of pictures for nine years, Walcamp committed suicide on this date in Los Angeles through an overdose of medication. She was forty-two. Interest in her career was resurrected by newfound attention to Weber's films.

NOVEMBER 18

1962—GOODNIGHT, IRENE

One of Hollywood's greatest fashion designers was in transit to a flakier state on this date—getting cremated for interment at Forest Lawn the following day. Known simply as "Irene," the former Irene Lentz Gibbons had checked into an eleventh-floor room at the Knickerbocker Hotel in Hollywood on November 15 and killed a bottle of Smirnoff and then herself. She jumped out the window and landed on the third-floor roof. As head fashion designer of MGM, succeeding the likewise mono-monikered Adrian, Irene had supervised attire design for Katharine Hepburn, Myrna Loy, Judy Garland, Elizabeth Taylor and many others. She had been caring for her stroke-paralyzed husband, Elliot Gibbons, brother of MGM production designer Cedric Gibbons and the screenwriter of such B pictures as *Storm over the Andes* (1935) and *Honolulu Lu* (1941). Irene's suicide note apologized for any inconvenience caused by the mess her passing would have made. She was sixty-one.

NOVEMBER 19

1954—SAMMY'S LIFE SAVED, EYEBALL LOST

On his way to becoming the most famous one-eyed black, Jewish, Republican singer-dancer-actor in history, Sammy Davis Jr. lost his left eyeball in the wee hours of this date on a highway outside San Bernardino, California. Sammy was returning to Hollywood from Las Vegas when he took over the driving duties from valet Charlie Head in Cajon Pass and promptly slammed into a stalled car in the middle of the highway. One of two women in the stalled car suffered a broken leg. Charlie's bridgework came loose. Sammy lost his car and his eye but retained his life to forge one of the most unique careers in American entertainment, including entry into Frank Sinatra's Rat Pack for nightclub shenanigans and the movies *Ocean's Eleven* (1960), *Sergeants 3* (1962) and *Robin and the 7 Hoods* (1964).

NOVEMBER 20

1980—THE HELL OF *HEAVEN'S GATE*

The day after the premiere of director Michael Cimino's 219-minute, $44 million *Heaven's Gate*, the reverberations were felt. "It fails so completely that you might suspect Mr. Cimino sold his soul to obtain the success of *The Deer Hunter* [1978] and the Devil has just come around to collect," wrote film critic Vincent Canby in the *New York Times*. United Artists pulled the movie from release after a week, cut it to 149 minutes and rereleased it in April 1981. Roger Ebert wrote in the *Chicago Sun-Times* that the recut movie was "the most scandalous cinematic waste I have ever seen, and remember, I've seen *Paint Your Wagon*." Swelled to four times its original $11 million budget, mostly by the demands of Cimino, *Heaven's Gate* closed its domestic theatrical run having grossed $1.3 million. *Final Cut: Art, Money, and Ego in the Making of Heaven's Gate, the Film That Sank United Artists* (1985) was written by UA executive Steven Bach. Parent company Transamerica Corp. exited the picture business. The film is credited with ending director-determined cinema, ushering in greater studio control.

NOVEMBER 21

1924—"MOVIE PRODUCER SHOT ON HEARST YACHT!"

William Randolph Hearst's yacht *The Oneida* set sail from San Pedro on November 15, 1924, bound for San Diego. Aboard were Hearst and his mistress, movie star Marion Davies, and half a dozen other actresses, as well as writers Louella O. Parsons and Elinor Glyn and Charlie Chaplin. The occasion was the birthday of studio head Thomas H. Ince, who joined the gang the next day via train. Two days later, the mercurial producer was hauled back up the coast by train and then ambulance to his Dias Dorados estate in Benedict Canyon, where he died. Ince's funeral was held on this date. The cause of death was listed as a heart attack. The early edition of the November 16, 1924 *Los Angeles Times* screamed the banner headline: "Movie Producer Shot on Hearst Yacht!" The story was pulled from later editions. Speculation was on a round fired by Hearst gunning after Chaplin, who supposedly romanced Davies on the sly. The newspaper tycoon's power and payoffs were such that the incident was conveniently erased. Parsons got a cushy syndicated column for the rest of her life. Ince Studios in Culver City was sold. Ince was forty-two.

NOVEMBER 22

1980—MGM: HOT, THEN ON FIRE

Metro-Goldwyn-Mayer was the hottest movie studio in the business through the mid-twentieth century. When the filmmaking giant got into the hospitality game, it became the hottest hotelier in Las Vegas. The MGM Grand Hotel became too hot on November 21, 1980, when it caught on fire and killed 85 people. The worst disaster in Nevada history also had the third-highest death toll of U.S. hotel fires. On this date, the day after the blaze, it was determined that more than 650 people were hurt, but most of the 5,000 people in the hotel escaped harm, about 1,000 of them evacuated off the roof by U.S. Special Operations helicopters, deployed from nearby Nellis Air Force Base. Most of the deaths were from smoke inhalation, one from burns and one from jumping. MGM fixed the place, sold it to Bally's Las Vegas and then built a new MGM Grand down the Strip.

NOVEMBER 23

1996—WOODY'S EXTRACURRICULAR ACTIVITIES

Woody Harrelson brought an air of extemporaneity to *Natural Born Killers* (1994), *The People vs. Larry Flynt* (1996), *No Country for Old Men* (2007) and to his time off as well. He was arrested on this date for climbing the Golden Gate Bridge with a banner protesting the logging of redwoods in Humboldt County, California. He was arrested in 1982 in Columbus, Ohio, for dancing in an intersection, after which he jumped out of a moving police van, kicked an officer and was found guilty of misdemeanor assault and resisting arrest. He was arrested in 1996 for planting marijuana seeds in Lee County, Kentucky, challenging a state law that didn't distinguish between marijuana and industrial hemp. A jury agreed with him. Felony charges for assaulting a photographer outside a Hollywood bar were dropped in 2006. Woody's chip on the shoulder may have to do with his father, Charles Harrelson, who earned two life sentences for the 1979 murder in San Antonio of Judge John Howland Wood, the only assassination of a federal judge in the twentieth century. Charles Harrelson died of a heart attack on March 15, 2007, in a federal maximum-security prison in Florence, Colorado. He was sixty-nine.

NOVEMBER 24

1958—PARKY, THERE'S NO TOMORROW!

The paterfamilias of the Beverly Hills Einsteins—rather than that wild-haired Viennese bunch—Harry Einstein was known as Parkyakarkus, Parky or Harry Parke, including in the movies *The Yanks Are Coming* (1942) and *Earl Carroll Vanities* (1945). The long moniker came from the Greek diner owner he played on Eddie Cantor's 1930s radio shows. During a performance on this date at the Friars Club Roast of Lucille Ball and Desi Arnaz, Einstein parked his carcass onto Milton Berle's shoulder. Uncle Miltie shrilly shouted, "Is there a doctor in the house?" Hilarity ensued and then ceased, as Einstein did. Berle told satin pipes Tony Martin to warble a diversion; the crooner sang "There's No Tomorrow." Impromptu, unsuccessful open-heart surgery was performed with a pen knife. Parky's showbiz genes carried on: his sons are the late screenwriter Charles Einstein, comic writer-director-actor Albert Brooks (aka Albert Einstein, not kidding) and the indestructible stunt comic Super Dave Osborne (aka Bob Einstein). Harry was fifty-four.

NOVEMBER 25

Cyril Ritchard had killed the crowd as a dynamic performer, killed characters as showy villains and then became one of the few actors to suffer the cause of his own end onstage. He acted in Alfred Hitchcock's *Blackmail* (1929) and Anthony Asquith's *The Winslow Boy* (1948), won Tony Awards for his Captain Hook in *Peter Pan* (1954) and *The Pleasure of His Company* (1959) and directed and performed in many musicals of 1950s television. He also japed the public as a *What's My Line?* panelist, answering to "Sir Cyril," although the aristocratic Australian was never knighted. He suffered a heart attack on this date while performing as the narrator in the Chicago touring company presentation of *Side by Side by Sondheim*. He survived a month in a coma, through his eightieth birthday, and died in a Chicago hospital. His funeral Mass was celebrated by another big TV star of the 1950s, Archbishop Fulton J. Sheen.

NOVEMBER 26

1980—SEXY REXY NOTCHES ANOTHER ONE

Rachel Roberts was divorced by Rex Harrison in 1971 and then drank and medicated her way to this date. The well-regarded British actress, who was nominated for an Oscar for Lindsay Anderson's *This Sporting Life* (1963) and also starred in *Murder on the Orient Express* (1974) and *Picnic at Hanging Rock* (1975), moved to Hollywood in 1975 to win Sexy Rexy back. Failing that, she flavored her last cocktail of booze and barbiturates with lye and alkali or another acidic substance. The poison caused death throes, which sent her through a glass divider in her home. Her severely cut and bloodied corpse was found by her gardener on her kitchen floor. She was fifty-three. Her ashes and those of her friend Jill Bennett were scattered on a melancholy boat trip on the River Thames in London, events filmed and eventually spliced into Anderson's *Is That All There Is?* (1994)—a "mock-umentary" on his own life.

NOVEMBER 27

1930—RAILROADED BY THE DA

Clara Bow's secretary was protective of the "It Girl's" savings, locking her in a power struggle with cowboy star and future Nevada lieutenant governor Rex Bell, Clara's future husband. Rex accused Daisy DeVoe of embezzling Bow's funds. Paramount's coziness with Los Angeles County district attorney Buron Fitts translated into the county grand jury indicting Daisy on this date on thirty-five counts of grand theft. Her sensational, press-blanketed 1931 trial found no proof of mishandled finances. The jury acquitted Daisy of thirty-four counts and found her guilty of one, involving an $825 check signed by Clara to pay income taxes. Sentenced to eighteen months in prison, Daisy told Fitts and Assistant DA David H. Clark, "You two are railroading me, and you'll both come to a bad end because of it." Four months later, Clark was charged with the shooting murders of LA racketeer Charles H. Crawford and journalist Herbert Spencer. Clark skated on both murders but went to prison for the 1953 shotgun slaying of the wife of his former law partner and died of a brain hemorrhage after a month in the joint. In 1973, Fitts blew his brains out with a pistol in Tulare County, California, a week after his seventy-eighth birthday.

NOVEMBER 28

1942—BUCK JONES AT THE COCOANUT GROVE

Western star Buck Jones sustained severe burns over most of his body on this date, perished on November 30 and was mourned throughout America. He was only the most notable victim of 492 people killed in Boston's Cocoanut Grove fire, the deadliest nightclub conflagration in U.S. history and the second-deadliest single-building blaze after the 1903 Iroquois Theater fire in Chicago, which killed 602. Born Charles Frederick Gebhart in Vincennes, Indiana, Jones was a U.S. cavalryman injured in the Moro Rebellion in the Philippines, cowboy in Oklahoma, "Wild West" show rider and five-dollar-a-day stuntman for Universal Pictures. Jones worked his way up to backup for Tom Mix and eventually starred in 160 pictures, including *White Eagle* (1932), *California Frontier* (1938) and *Riders of the West* (1942). Jones was the guest of honor at the Cocoanut Grove at a party thrown by Monogram producer Scott R. Dunlap, who survived the blaze. Jones was fifty.

NOVEMBER 29

1981—NATALIE WOOD'S CATALINA DIP

The body of Natalie Wood was found on this date on a remote portion of the rocky, rugged seashore of Santa Catalina Island. She had gone to the island for a weekend aboard a yacht with her husband, Robert Wagner, and her costar in *Brainstorm* (released in 1983), Christopher Walken, along with the boat's captain, Dennis Davern. Los Angeles County coroner Thomas Noguchi originally ruled her death a drowning accident. Natalie couldn't swim. She had been drinking, and her autopsy showed drugs in her system, including Darvon. Speculation centered on a Wagner-Walken argument that night over the charms of the star of *Rebel Without a Cause* (1955), *West Side Story* (1961) and *Splendor in the Grass* (1961). The case was reopened in 2011, and the cause of death was now "undetermined" instead of accidental because the bruises on her body were inconsistent with a drowning death. Her funeral was attended by Frank Sinatra, Rock Hudson, Laurence Olivier and other Hollywood royalty. Natalie was forty-three.

NOVEMBER 30

1923—MATCHING WARDROBE

In one of the notable film-set tragedies of the silent era, smoking killed Martha Mansfield in San Antonio, Texas, on this day. She had worked her way up from supporting roles in films starring Max Linder and John Barrymore to the leading lady in the Civil War drama *The Warrens of Virginia* (1923), based on a play by Cecil B. De Mille's brother, William C. De Mille. On the set, an actor tossed away a smoker's match, and it ignited Mansfield's Civil War–era costume of hoopskirts and ruffles. The flames soon consumed her clothes. Star Wilfred Lytell threw an overcoat over her, protecting her face. Others were burned trying to remove her flaming garb. Mansfield was rushed to a hospital, where she died the following day from her burns. She was twenty-four.

DECEMBER 1

The silent era's more provocative foreign films include director G.W. Pabst's *Pandora's Box*, about Lulu, a beautiful dancer-cum-prostitute whose insouciant sexuality captivates men and women, leading to a botched wedding, sensational murder trial and eventually her debauchery's severe antidote, Jack the Ripper. The pre–Production Code film, which opened in New York on this date, was resurrected by revisionist criticism, partly because of its presentation of Lulu's amorality but mostly because it issued through the hypnotic performance of Louise Brooks, one of the more unconventional stars. Her Page Boy haircut, dark beauty and placid glide through the jealous paroxysms she causes imbue Lulu with a mesmerizing aspect. Unwilling to conform to Hollywood's typecasting, Cherryvale, Kansas native Brooks worked in Europe, including in Pabst's *Diary of a Lost Girl* (1929). She was offered only small parts back in Hollywood, and her final film was a John Wayne B western, *Overland Stage Raiders* (1938). Brooks died on August 8, 1985, in Rochester, New York. She was seventy-eight.

DECEMBER 2

Subtitled "400 Truths about the World's Greatest Human," this Gotham/Penguin paperback authored by Ian Spector was in its first week of release on this date. The book promulgated a wide-ranging list of absurd abilities alleged to be possessed by the martial arts–prone star of *Walker, Texas Ranger* and movies including *Missing in Action* (1984), *The Delta Force* (1986) and, later, *The Expendables 2* (2012). The "facts" in the book include that Chuck counted to infinity twice, he urinates his name into concrete the way kids do in snow, his tears cure cancer but he's never wept, he slams revolving doors and he ties his shoes with his feet. The book contends that Chuck's main export is pain and that cobras die an agonizing death after biting Chuck. The star sued Penguin and Spector this month for trademark infringement, unjust enrichment and privacy rights. But the Chuck-ster eventually went along with the gags and withdrew the suit in May 2008. Spector wrote several sequels. One contends that when Chuck Norris tells time, time obeys.

DECEMBER 3

Jason Priestley was tooling home from a concert in the wee hours of this date when he drove his Porsche into a light pole, trash cans and a parked car near the corner of Canyon Drive and Franklin Avenue in Hollywood. A passenger in the car suffered a broken arm. The star of such television series as *Beverly Hills 90210* and, in this century, *Call Me Fitz* and such films as *Tombstone* (1993), *Eye of the Beholder* (1999) and *Going the Distance* (2004) told police he had swerved to avoid hitting a deer, a legitimate hazard in the Hollywood Hills. But the LAPD arrested him anyway for drunk driving. He later pleaded no contest and was sentenced to five days in a work-release jail program. The Vancouver-born actor had just directed the well-received documentary *Barenaked in America* (1999) about the band Barenaked Ladies.

DECEMBER 4

1988—BUSEY'S LOST CAUSE, SALVAGED LIFE

About a month after lobbying against a then-proposed (and eventually enacted) state law for motorcyclists to wear mandatory protective helmets, actor Gary Busey was driving a Harley-Davidson west on Washington Boulevard near Robertson Boulevard in Culver City when he was thrown off his ride and his head struck a curb. He wasn't wearing a helmet. He was rushed to Cedars-Sinai Medical Center with a fractured skull; physicians performed neurosurgery. Busey, then forty-four, was in intensive care for several days. He had appeared at a benefit sponsored by the California Motorcyclist Association a month earlier at North Hollywood's Palomino Club to raise money for lobbyists to fight the mandatory-helmet bill. An Oscar nominee for *The Buddy Holly Story* (1978), Busey has been ubiquitous in films and television before and after the accident, but the damage was diagnosed as permanent.

DECEMBER 5

The June 2009 death of the former lover of Rock Hudson, Marc Christian MacGinnis, was announced on this date by MacGinnis's sister, Susan Dahl. MacGinnis, who went by Christian, his mother's maiden name, won a multimillion-dollar settlement in 1991 from the actor's estate after a jury agreed that Rock had knowingly exposed him to AIDS. Christian died of pulmonary complications on June 2 at Providence Saint Joseph Medical Center in Burbank. Christian had sued Hudson's estate and former secretary Mark Miller for $10 million, saying that he suffered severe emotional distress hearing that Hudson, the star of more than one hundred films and television shows, had AIDS. In 1989, a Los Angeles County Superior Court jury concluded that Hudson displayed "outrageous conduct" and awarded Christian $21.75 million in damages, later reduced to $5.5 million and upheld by a state appellate court. Christian was fifty-six.

DECEMBER 6

1971—TOM NEAL'S DEAD-END DETOUR

In the early morning hours of April 2, 1965, Tom Neal shot his third wife, the former Gale Bennett, in the back of the head in their Palm Springs home. The Riverside County grand jury indicted him for murder, but he eventually was convicted of involuntary manslaughter and received a ten-year sentence. He was paroled on this date after serving only six years. Neal died less than a year later, on August 7, 1972, in North Hollywood, of heart failure. He was fifty-eight. Hollywood gave him a B-movie career, and he made the most of it—in director Edgar G. Ulmer's classic film noir *Detour* (1945), as well as *Another Thin Man* (1939), *Bowery at Midnight* (1942), *I Shot Billy the Kid* (1950) and others. He was blackballed out of Hollywood after a September 13, 1951 fistfight with star Franchot Tone over the affections of actress Barbara Payton. Neal moved to Palm Springs and became a gardener. His second wife died of cancer, the third from his handgun.

The famous extended rear-seat driving shot in director Edgar G. Ulmer's *Detour* (1945) featured Ann Savage and Tom Neal.

DECEMBER 7

Few great character actors have been as beloved as Harry Morgan. In more than one hundred films or TV movies and as a regular on eight television series—memorably as LAPD Officer Bill Gannon in *Dragnet* and as Colonel Sherman T. Potter in *M*A*S*H*—Harry often was more familiar than stars billed above him. His classics include *The Ox-Bow Incident* (1943), *High Noon* (1952) and *Inherit the Wind* (1960). He died of pneumonia on this date at the age of ninety-six, but not before achieving notoriety as a rare octogenarian spousal abuser. On July 2, 1996, Harry's second wife, Barbara, then seventy, called 911. The LAPD arrived at their Brentwood home to find her with a swollen left foot, gash near her right eye and bruised right arm. Morgan, then eighty-one, was arrested and released on $5,000 bail. Barbara was treated by paramedics and taken to a hospital for observation. The charges were dropped, and the couple remained together for the rest of his life.

DECEMBER 8

1963—Frank Sinatra Jr.: Kidnapped by Amateurs

Then nineteen and aping dear old dad as the singer fronting the Tommy Dorsey orchestra, Frank Sinatra Jr. became one of the most famous kidnap victims in American crime lore when three clods ordered him at gunpoint into a car on this date at Harrah's Lake Tahoe. He was released two days later when Francis Albert Sr. shelled out the $240,000 demanded by the cheap kidnappers. The FBI nabbed the geniuses after a couple of days. The "mastermind" behind this farrago, one Barry Keenan, was sentenced to life plus seventy-five years but was back in society before he served five years on the contention that he was insane when he dreamed up the scheme. Frank Sr. was suspected of cooking up the plot to get the boy some publicity and forever resented the accusation. Frank Jr. went on to have an un-singular career.

DECEMBER 9

2008—RICHIE RICH'S FORTUNES

The most successful child actor after Shirley Temple, reportedly making $8 million a movie, Macaulay Culkin starred in the *Home Alone* franchise, *Richie Rich* (1994) and other pictures. After Mac became a cash kid, his dad, Kit Culkin, divorced his mom, Patricia, and claimed ownership of the kid's fortune. The Manhattan Supreme Court said otherwise, and Mac became estranged from his father. Two days before Christmas 1998, four people died in a fire that was started by a faulty heater in Patricia's Manhattan flat; Mac and Patricia were sued. On September 17, 2004, Mac was arrested in Oklahoma City for the possession of marijuana; after reversing his plea to guilty, Mac received three one-year suspended prison terms and was ordered to pay $540 in fees. Mac testified at the 2005 trial of Michael Jackson that the suggestion of any inappropriate sexual behavior toward Mac by the singer was "absolutely ridiculous." On this date, Mac's sister, Dakota Culkin, was hit by a car in Los Angeles and died from her injuries the following day at UCLA Medical Center; she was twenty-nine. As this book goes to print, Mac is thirty-two.

DECEMBER 10

2007—SIZEMORE OUT OF THE BUCKET

Tom Sizemore was released from a Kern County, California prison on this date after being awarded 213 days' credit for time already spent in jail or rehab for quite a few bad cocktails over the dam. On August 15, 2003, Sizemore, who memorably played the sergeant in *Saving Private Ryan* (1998) and was ubiquitous in films—*Striking Distance* (1993), *Natural Born Killers* (1994), etc.—was convicted on six of the sixteen charges filed against him by Heidi Fleiss, including domestic abuse, death threats, harassment and vandalism. After her "Hollywood Madam" scandal rocked LA through the 1990s, the drug-plagued Heidi played house with drug-plagued Tommy. His sentence in the Heidi raps was reduced to ninety days, plus counseling. Sizemore was arrested in West Hollywood on drug possession charges and for parole violation and sexual harassment in 2004 and then on methamphetamine possession in Bakersfield, leading to the Kern County cooler. Old pal Robert De Niro once showed up at Sizemore's doorstep with Sizemore's mom and gave him an ultimatum: jail or rehab. He chose rehab.

DECEMBER 11

1990—COREY'S DRUG ESCAPADES

Corey Feldman, star of *Gremlins* (1984), *Stand by Me* (1986), *Bordello of Blood* (1996) and half a dozen TV series including *Dweebs* and *Splatter*, escaped heavy drug-trafficking charges and skated away from jail time on December 10, 1990. The news hit the media on this date that, instead, he was sentenced to four years' probation and fined $5,000 in a plea bargain with the district attorney's office related to possession arrests. He pleaded no contest to two charges of heroin possession and one of cocaine possession. In exchange, prosecutors agreed to dismiss felony charges of heroin possession for sale and transportation of heroin. Then nineteen, Feldman agreed to finish a seven-month drug rehabilitation program, which he entered in October 1989. VH1 once ranked him eighth among the 100 Greatest Kid Stars.

DECEMBER 12

2001—WINONA SACKED AT SAKS FIFTH AVENUE

Winona Ryder was arrested on shoplifting charges on this date, accused of stealing $5,500 worth of designer clothes and accessories at Saks Fifth Avenue in Beverly Hills. Los Angeles County district attorney Stephen Cooley threw the book at the petite actress; his team of eight prosecutors filed four felony charges against the star of *Edward Scissorhands* (1990) and *The Age of Innocence* (1993). Ryder was convicted of grand theft, shoplifting and vandalism but was acquitted of burglary. In December 2002, she was sentenced to three years' probation, 480 hours of community service, $3,700 in fines and $6,355 in restitution to Saks and ordered to attend psychological and drug counseling. Superior Court judge Elden Fox noted that Ryder served her allotment of community service, and in June 2004, the felonies were reduced to misdemeanors. Ryder remained on probation until December 2005.

DECEMBER 13

Walter Wanger (as in "ranger"), who had produced John Ford's *Stagecoach* (1940) and Alfred Hitchcock's *Foreign Correspondent* (1940), infamously shot his wife's agent, Jennings Lang, in the groin on this date in a Beverly Hills parking lot. Lang and Wanger's wife, Joan Bennett, the star of *The Woman in the Window* (1944), *The Reckless Moment* (1949) and *Father of the Bride* (1950), had been conducting a tryst. The shooting and aftermath were sensationalized by the press, and eventually Hollywood lawyer-to-the-stars Jerry Geisler had Wanger plead temporary insanity. The producer was sentenced to four months in the clink. Lang recovered to become a producer of group-jeopardy disaster epics: *Airport 1975* (1974) and *Earthquake* (1974). Wanger produced *Riot in Cell Block 11* (1954) based on his incarceration. Bennett starred in the TV series *Dark Shadows*. And Billy Wilder wrote, directed and produced the Academy Award–winning best picture *The Apartment* (1960), inspired by the Bennett-Lang affair.

Joan Bennett (left) starred with Dan Duryea in *Scarlet Street* (1945).

DECEMBER 14

1944—"MEXICAN SPITFIRE'S" SUICIDE

One of the few south-of-the-border stars of early Hollywood, Maria Guadalupe Villalobos Velez, aka Lupe Velez, from San Luis de Potosi, Mexico, starred opposite Douglas Fairbanks in *The Gaucho* (1927), Gary Cooper in *The Wolf Song* (1929) and other pictures. Lupe's affairs included those with Cooper, John Gilbert, Charlie Chaplin, Errol Flynn and Johnny Weissmuller. She and *Tarzan* star Weissmuller were married for five tempestuous years. Her character of the "Mexican Spitfire" was popular in *The Girl from Mexico* (1939) and then *Mexican Spitfire* (1940) and sequels. The Catholic Lupe became pregnant with actor Harald Maresch's child and refused to have the baby out of wedlock. Her final note read: "To Harald: May God forgive you and forgive me, too; but I prefer to take my life away and our baby's, before I bring him with shame, or killin' [*sic*] him.—Lupe." She ingested eighty Seconal pills and expired on her bed, surrounded by flowers. She was thirty-six.

DECEMBER 15

1955—Rat Pack: Bogie Squeals to Scribbler

Journalist Joe Hyams listened to Humphrey Bogart's amusing tale of his partying pals and published it for posterity on this date in the *New York Herald-Tribune*. The back story goes that on a Vegas bender in June that year, the lisping tough-guy star of *Casablanca* (1943), *The African Queen* (1951) and other classics and his soused pals—Frank Sinatra, Judy Garland, David Niven, Angie Dickinson, Martha Hyer, musician Jimmy Van Heusen and restaurateur Mike Romanoff—were assessed by Mrs. Bogart, Lauren Bacall, who cracked,

"You look like a goddamn rat pack!" It broke up the joint and stuck as a moniker. After Bogie died of cancer in 1957, the king-rat status shifted by rote to Frank, with whom the Pack's notoriety was ring-a-ding-dinged into pop culture lore in the 1960s with Dean Martin, Sammy Davis Jr., Peter Lawford and Joey Bishop.

The original *Ocean's Eleven* (1960) featured (from left) Dean Martin, Frank Sinatra, Sammy Davis Jr., Joey Bishop, Peter Lawford and Angie Dickinson.

DECEMBER 16

1935—THELMA TODD AND THE MOB

Thelma Todd was Miss Massachusetts of 1925 and acted in the first version of *The Maltese Falcon* (1931), starring Ricardo Cortez; with the Marx brothers in *Monkey Business* (1931) and *Horse Feathers* (1932); and with John Barrymore in *Counsellor at Law* (1933). She was found dead in her car inside the garage of actress Jewel Carmen, the former wife of Roland West, Todd's lover. Carmen's house was approximately a block from Thelma Todd's Sidewalk Café in Pacific Palisades. The cause of death was carbon monoxide poisoning. She had spent the previous night at the Trocadero nightclub, arguing with her ex-husband, racketeer Pat DiCicco, Hollywood emissary of Lucky Luciano. LAPD investigators ruled the death accidental, but the Los Angeles County grand jury called it a suicide. Rumors said extortion, and blood was supposedly on her face and dress. Her body was quickly cremated. Thelma was twenty-nine.

DECEMBER 17

1980—SIR LARRY AND ALL THAT JAZZ

When Al Jolson played *The Jazz Singer* (1927), a groundbreaking movie for the use of sound in motion pictures, its source play by Samson Raphaelson, about a cantor who defies his orthodox Jewish father to become the title crooner, was already moldy stuff. The 1952 remake with Danny Thomas and the 1960 TV version with Jerry Lewis were considered left of ludicrous. When non-actor Neil Diamond tried the part in the 1980 remake, released on this date, the result was an unconscionable glop of tacky schmaltz on stale matzo balls. Pairing the romance balladeer with Laurence Olivier as the father was like a tumbleweed rolling past a sequoia. At the annual Golden Raspberry Awards naming the movie year's worst offerings, Neil was named worst actor and Olivier worst supporting actor. A singular distinction for most, but not for Sir Larry; his undiscerning period brought the Razzie for worst actor the following year for his General Douglas MacArthur in *Inchon*.

DECEMBER 18

1956—"DIRTIEST AMERICAN-MADE" MOVIE

One of the few films approved by the Production Code but condemned by the National Legion of Decency was released on this date. Director Elia Kazan's *Baby Doll* (1956), based on the Tennessee Williams play *27 Wagons Full of Cotton*, starred Carroll Baker as the teenage wife of middle-aged Mississippi farmer Karl Malden. The arranged marriage is scheduled to be consummated in three days, on Baby Doll's twentieth birthday. Baby Doll sleeps in a crib, sucking her thumb—the film's poster art—and also is lasciviously pursued by a tireless swain (Eli Wallach). The Legion of Decency claimed the picture was "grievously offensive to Christian and traditional standards of morality and decency." The legion succeeded in having it withdrawn from most U.S. theaters. *Time* magazine helped the crusade, calling *Baby Doll* the "dirtiest American-made motion picture that had ever been legally exhibited." The film received four Oscar nominations, including for Baker for best actress and Williams for best screenplay.

DECEMBER 19

Robert Altman's *Popeye* entered its second week of release on this date to a middling box-office take that would reach $25 million in domestic rentals after costing $23 million to make on location over a year's time on the island of Malta. The perception exists that the film is a full-scale financial bomb instead of a break-even artistic failure because Altman's live-action version about the cartoon sailor is oddly uninvolving, even with Robin Williams in the title role. What's more, the film's miserable musical numbers are as memorable as toothpaste jingles. Paramount sued Altman after the fact because the picture nearly doubled its original $13 million budget. Producer Bob Evans skated away to an even more ridiculous fiasco, *The Cotton Club* (1984). The experience taught Williams to never become a director. "It would be difficult," Williams said, "for me to say to someone, 'I'm sorry, you know that wasn't very good,' and then have them go, 'Well, what about *Popeye*?'"

DECEMBER 20

2009—BRITTANY DOA, THEN HUBBY

The Los Angeles Fire Department responded to a call on this date from the Hollywood Hills home of actress Brittany Murphy and her husband, British-born screenwriter Simon Monjack. She had collapsed in a bathroom, and firefighters attempted to resuscitate her. The star of *Drop Dead Gorgeous* (1999), *Girl, Interrupted* (1999), *Riding in Cars with Boys* (2002), *Sin City* (2005) and other films was transported to Cedars-Sinai Medical Center, where she was pronounced dead from cardiac arrest. The Los Angeles County coroner concluded that Brittany's cause of death was pneumonia. She also had an iron deficiency and levels of cold-fighting, over-the-counter drugs in her system. Her death was ruled an accident. She was buried at Forest Lawn Hollywood Hills on Christmas Eve 2009. On May 23, 2010, widower Monjack was found dead in the same residence. The coroner ruled that he died of pneumonia and anemia. Brittany was thirty-two, Monjack forty.

DECEMBER 21

2002—AND THE OSCAR GOES TO...THE HIGHEST BIDDER!

Steven Spielberg rescued the late Bette Davis's first Oscar from the auction block when he paid $180,000 plus fees and taxes on this date for the legendary performer's best actress Oscar for *Dangerous* (1935). The year before, Spielberg, whose Oscars include those for best picture for *Schindler's List* (1992) and best director for that film and *Saving Private Ryan* (1998), had bought Davis's second Oscar, for *Jezebel* (1938), for $578,000. Spielberg returned the awards to the Academy of Motion Picture Arts & Sciences. To stem Oscar-trafficking, the academy requires winners to sign an agreement to return statuettes to the academy for $1 apiece if they wish to part with them. But Sotheby's sold the best picture Oscar for *Gone with the Wind* (1939) to Michael Jackson for a record $1.5 million. Magician David Copperfield keeps Michael Curtiz's best director Oscar for *Casablanca* (1943) in his bedroom. "Objects should be where they do the most good," Copperfield said. He bought it in 2003 for $232,000.

DECEMBER 22

1964—WILDER YET: *KISS ME, STUPID!*

Billy Wilder, whose masterful writing and directing had smartly crafted innuendo into films for several generations, left suggestion to the wind with *Kiss Me, Stupid!* His sleaziest picture and a shocker for early 1960s audiences, the film was released on this date. Dean Martin plays Dino, a boozy famous singer who needs to "have a woman" each night or he gets a headache. In Climax, Nevada, locals sabotage his car and scheme to have him listen to their tunes to take them to Hollywood. Kim Novak plays hooker Polly the Pistol. Dino and Zelda Spooner (Felicia Farr, Jack Lemmon's then-wife) get crocked at the Belly Button Bar. Satirizing himself as a come-what-may booze-hound and womanizer, the real Dino was amid his Rat Pack years, strolling through Wilder's Twentynine Palms, California sets as if the cameras weren't turned on. The National Legion of Decency condemned the film, and critics dismissed it. The *Variety* critic opined that Wilder "has directed with frontal assault rather than suggestive finesse."

DECEMBER 23

1997—LIKE BELUSHI, LIKE FARLEY

Portly comedian Chris Farley followed John Belushi's career and in his footsteps at Second City in Chicago and the Not Ready for Primetime Players on NBC's *Saturday Night Live!* Chris followed through on becoming a film star, in *Tommy Boy* (1995), *Black Sheep* (1996) and *Beverly Hills Ninja* (1997). His excesses mirrored Belushi's. On the day of his death, December 18, 1997, after a year of seeking antidotes to his obesity and drug addiction, Farley had been awake for four days and spent his last one in the company of a hooker, who left him on the floor of his Chicago apartment. His brother John found him the next day, still on the floor. Like Belushi, Farley died from a "speedball," an overdose of heroin and cocaine. A funeral Mass was held on this date at Our Lady Queen of Peace Roman Catholic Church in Madison, Wisconsin. The more than five hundred attendees included Lorne Michaels, Dan Aykroyd, John Goodman, Tom Arnold, Chris Rock, Adam Sandler, George Wendt and Rob Schneider. Like Belushi, Farley was thirty-three.

DECEMBER 24

1940—HEDY LAMARR'S SKINNY-DIPPING

Director Gustav Machatý's *Ecstasy* (1933) was notable for its scenes of Hedy Lamarr swimming nude and those depicting sexual intercourse, including a female orgasm, via the actors' faces. *Ecstasy* was one of the first foreign films to be condemned by the National Legion of Decency, in 1940. The U.S. distributor lobbied the Motion Picture Producers and Distributors of America to get a seal of approval. But Joseph I. Breen, censor of the Production Code Administration, called the picture "highly—even dangerously—indecent" in a memo to Will H. Hays, president of the MPPDA. Hays told the producers: "We cannot approve your production *Ecstasy*...it is a [story] of illicit love and frustrated sex, treated in detail without sufficient compensating moral values." Without the approval, *Ecstasy* opened on this date in a few indie houses. Most states demanded scenes be cut. Pennsylvania banned it.

DECEMBER 25

The versatility of Charlie is such that he can be garden-variety hammered, all gooned up and out of his freaking gourd at any time, including on Christmas. After he pulled a knife on his wife, actress Brooke Mueller, at their Colorado home, Charlie was whisked to the Pitkin County Jail in Aspen for an eight-hour incarceration. He was released on $8,500 bail and charged with felony menacing, third-degree assault and criminal mischief. In August 2010, Sheen was convicted of misdemeanor assault and sentenced to a month in rehab, a month's probation and thirty-six hours of anger management. Charlie eventually filed for divorce from the mother of his twins and the stepmother of his two other children. He subsequently starred in the sitcom *Anger Management*.

DECEMBER 26

By this annual date of post-Christmas redux, most of Sharon Stone's gift watches to the eighty-two members of the Hollywood Foreign Press Association should have been returned to USA Films. Stone had starred in writer-director Albert Brooks's *The Muse* (1999), playing the ethereal "Zeus's Daughter," an inspiration and then headache for a struggling screenwriter (played by Brooks). To influence the HFPA into a Golden Globe nomination for Stone's performance in *The Muse*, publicists had shipped each of the HFPA members a Coach watch valued at between $295 and $395. On December 13, HFPA president Helmut Voss ordered his minions to return the timepieces. "This watch was way, way, way beyond the edge of the envelope as far as promotional considerations, like T-shirts," said Voss. "This is definitely a no-no for a group like ours that wants to protect the integrity of its award." Integrity had been lacking in past episodes of HFPA influence-peddling.

DECEMBER 27

1990—*THE BONFIRE OF THE VANITIES*

Of all the star-studded duds in Hollywood history, few crashed and burned like *The Bonfire of the Vanities*, the adaptation of Tom Wolfe's satirical novel about the racial and political hot potato of an inner-city accident in which a Wall Street financier's mistress hits a boy with his car. Michael Cristofer adapted the book for director Brian De Palma, whose cast included Tom Hanks, Bruce Willis, Melanie Griffith, Morgan Freeman, F. Murray Abraham, Kim Cattrall, Alan King, Kirsten Dunst, Saul Rubinek and Robert Stephens. Julie Salamon's book about the picture, *The Devil's Candy: The Bonfire of the Vanities Goes to Hollywood* (1991), reissued as *The Devil's Candy: The Anatomy of a Hollywood Fiasco*, details the $47 million movie's making and aftermath, which, by this date, the end of its first week in release, was obviously shaping up as an all-time box-office bomb. The film earned $15 million in domestic exhibition for Warner Bros.

DECEMBER 28

Pre–Lindsay Lohan, Shannen Doherty was briefly the Hollywood transgressor chick du jour. In 1996, she smashed a bottle on a car in Beverly Hills, was put on probation and was ordered into anger-management counseling. On this date, at 3:00 a.m., she drove her pickup truck erratically across lanes on the freeway. The California Highway Patrol took notice. The former *Playboy* model and star of such television series as *Beverly Hills 90210* and *Charmed* and such films as *Sleeping with the Devil* (1997) and *Satan's School for Girls* (2000) was headed to her Ventura County ranch. Her blood-alcohol level was over California's legal limit of 0.08. She was escorted to the sheriff's holding cell for ten hours of sober thought. Her sentencing included an order to deliver talks to teens on the evils of drunk driving, pay a $1,500 fine and complete three years' probation.

DECEMBER 29

Christian Slater guzzled a few pops and led police on a drunken car chase that ended, vehicle-wise, on this date with a crash into a West Hollywood utility pole. The star of *Heathers* (1988), *Broken Arrow* (1996), *Windtalkers* (2002) and other movies supposedly kicked a cop with his cowboy boots after getting out of the car. He also tried to jump a fence. He was charged with evading police, driving under the influence, assault with a deadly weapon (boots) and driving with a suspended license. He spent ten days in jail. Slater's brushes with the law include illegal gun possession at New York's JFK Airport in 1994; a 1997 drunken attack on his girlfriend; a mêlée during which he allegedly bit another guy; and playing grab-ass in 2005, which translated as third-degree abuse.

DECEMBER 30

1953—*THE WILD ONE* LOOSE IN NEW YORK!

Marlon Brando won Oscars for *On the Waterfront* (1954) and *The Godfather* (1972) and was acclaimed for his work in *A Streetcar Named Desire* (1950), *Julius Caesar* (1953) and many other films. But the most iconic image of the 1950s' new catnip for women—this nasal-mumbling scratcher with the animal magnetism and rebel-youth rep—comes from *The Wild One* (1954), which was released in New York on this date. While he revolutionized American screen acting as the prime Method performer in films, he was seen, as many new things are, as a menace and threat to the status quo. In *The Wild One*, Brando plays the leather-jacketed leader of a motorcycle gang terrorizing a small California community. His at-first nihilistic character is asked, "Hey, Johnny, what are you rebelling against?" And he responds, "Whadda ya got?" His alley-cat wooing of Mary Murphy, macho standoffs with the grungy Lee Marvin and slouchy beer bottle swilling have passed from this picture into pop-culture lore.

DECEMBER 31

1971—DUEL LOSES DUEL WITH HIMSELF

In the early morning hours of this date, after watching on television his own show, *Alias Smith and Jones*, Pete Duel went into the bedroom of his home on Glen Green Terrace in the Hollywood Hills, picked up his .38 pistol, returned to the living room and shot himself to death. Pete had been a regular on *Gidget* with Sally Field and had costarred with Rod Taylor in *The Hell with Heroes* (1968) and George Peppard in *Cannon for Cordoba* (1971). It was said that he wanted to stretch beyond sidekick status. He had used the same .38 a week before his end to shoot the notice that explained he lost a Screen Actors Guild election. Pete's brother, Geoffrey Deuel, used the family's surname spelling when he costarred as Billy the Kid with John Wayne in *Chisum* (1969). Peter is buried near his family's home in Monroe County, New York. He was thirty-one.

Selected Bibliography

BOOKS

Anger, Kenneth. *Hollywood Babylon*. San Francisco: Straight Arrow Press, 1975.*

———. *Hollywood Babylon II*. New York: E.P. Dutton, 1984.*

Brooks, Tim, and Earle Marsh. *The Complete Directory of Primetime Network TV Shows, 1946-Present* (Fourth Edition). New York: Ballantine, 1988.

Katz, Ephraim. *The Film Encyclopedia*. New York: HarperPerennial, 1998.

Parish, James Robert. *Fiasco: A History of Hollywood's Iconic Flops*. Hoboken, NJ: John & Wiley & Sons, 2006.

———. *Hollywood Bad Boys*. New York: McGraw-Hill, 2002.

———. *The Hollywood Book of Break-Ups*. Hoboken, NJ: John Wiley & Sons, 2006.

———. *The Hollywood Book of Death*. New York: Contemporary Books, 2001.

———. *The Hollywood Book of Extravagance*. Hoboken, NJ: John Wiley & Sons, 2007.

———. *The Hollywood Book of Love*. New York: McGraw-Hill, 2003.

———. *The Hollywood Book of Scandals*. New York: McGraw-Hill, 2004.

*The veracity of the Anger books has been questioned by historians, but they were pioneering volumes, and most of their occasionally disputed tales are factually based.

WEBSITES

www.findadeath.com
www.findagrave.com
www.history.com
www.historyorb.com
www.imdb.com
www.nndb.com
www.on-this-day.com
www.seeing-stars.com

PERIODICALS

Chicago Sun-Times
Daily/Weekly Variety
The Hollywood Reporter
LA Weekly
Los Angeles Times
New York Daily News
New York Post
New York Times
People Weekly
San Francisco Chronicle

About the Author

Jerry Roberts has authored or been credited editor on sixteen books for nine publishers. His last book was *The Complete History of American Film Criticism* (2010) for Santa Monica Press. He's a commissioning editor for The History Press and acquires books on local and regional history. He is senior editor for the Catalina Island Conservancy. Roberts formerly was an acquisitions editor for Arcadia Publishing. His books include *Mitchum: In His Own Words* and *The Great American Playwrights on the Screen*.

For eleven years, Roberts was film critic for Copley Los Angeles Newspapers and a columnist for San Diego–based Copley News Service. He has written thousands of articles and reviews on film and television, including for *Daily Variety*, *The Hollywood Reporter* and the former *DGA Magazine*. Roberts formerly was a news reporter for the *Pittsburgh Post-Gazette* and served as sports editor for three other Pennsylvania newspapers. A native of Kittanning, Pennsylvania, he lives with his wife, Joanne, in Carson, California.

VISIT US AT
WWW.HISTORYPRESS.NET